Recommended D

A checklist of human rights must include basic housing, universal healthcare, equitable funding for public schools, and tuition-free college and vocational training.

In addition to the basics, though, we need much more to fully thrive. Subsidized childcare, universal pre-K, a universal basic income, subsidized high-speed internet, net neutrality, fare-free public transit (plus *more* public transit), and medically assisted death for the terminally ill who want it.

None of this will matter, though, if we neglect to address the rapidly worsening climate crisis.

Sound expensive? It is.

But not as expensive as refusing to implement these changes. The cost of climate disasters each year has grown to staggering figures. And the cost of social and political upheaval from not meeting the needs of suffering workers, families, and individuals may surpass even that.

It's best we understand that the vast sums required to enact meaningful change are an investment which will pay off not only in some indeterminate future but in fact almost immediately. And without these adjustments to our lifestyles and values, there may very well not be a future capable of sustaining freedom and democracy…or even civilization itself.

Praise for Johnny Townsend

In *Zombies for Jesus*, "Townsend isn't writing satire, but deeply emotional and revealing portraits of people who are, with a few exceptions, quite lovable."

Kel Munger, *Sacramento News and Review*

In *Sex among the Saints,* "Townsend writes with a deadpan wit and a supple, realistic prose that's full of psychological empathy….he takes his protagonists' moral struggles seriously and invests them with real emotional resonance."

Kirkus Reviews

Let the Faggots Burn: The UpStairs Lounge Fire is "a gripping account of all the horrors that transpired that night, as well as a respectful remembrance of the victims."

Terry Firma, Patheos

"Johnny Townsend's 'Partying with St. Roch' [in the anthology *Latter-Gay Saints*] tells a beautiful, haunting tale."

Kent Brintnall, Out in Print: Queer Book Reviews

Selling the City of Enoch is "sharply intelligent…pleasingly complex…The stories are full of…doubters, but there's no vindictiveness in these pages; the characters continuously poke holes in Mormonism's more extravagant absurdities, but they take very little pleasure in doing so….Many of Townsend's stories…have a provocative edge to them, but this [book] displays a great deal of insight as well…a playful, biting and surprisingly warm collection."

Kirkus Reviews

Gayrabian Nights is "an allegorical tour de force…a hard-core emotional punch."

Gay. Guy. Reading and Friends

The Washing of Brains has "A lovely writing style, and each story [is] full of unique, engaging characters….immensely entertaining."

Rainbow Awards

In *Dead Mankind Walking*, "Townsend writes in an energetic prose that balances crankiness and humor….A rambunctious volume of short, well-crafted essays…"

Kirkus Reviews

Recommended Daily Humanity

Johnny Townsend

Print ISBN: 979-8-9877113-0-9

Printed on acid-free paper.

2023

First Edition

Cover by BetiBup33 Studio Design

Special thanks to Donna Banta
for her editorial assistance

For more of Donna's own work,
please read *Seer Stone* and *False Prophet.*

Contents

We Must Adjust to a Changing World....10
Moral Snobbery, Snarky Comments, and Mockery Rarely Win Converts....14
From Book Burner to Librarian....19
I'm My Own Grandchild....27
The Party That Cried Wolf....31
Let's Change Our Attitude Toward Race....35
Student Loans Create Chronic Stress....40
Every Newscast Must Discuss Climate....44
Second Thought: An Introductory Socialist YouTube Channel to Share with Friends and Family....49
Weekend and Holiday Transit Schedules Hurt the Most Vulnerable Riders....53
Pro-Corporate Programming as 'Feel Good' Drama....58
Will Capitalism Reign During the Millennium?....62
Homeless Sweeps and Seattle's Lack of Compassion....66
Disdain for the Deluded....71
COVID Analogies Are the New Holocaust Analogies....77
Are We 'Catastrophizing' if We're Really in a Catastrophe?....81
Workers Quitting Crappy Jobs Should Also Quit Crappy Political Parties....86
Go Fund Yourself!....91
A Tale of Two Parties....96
Stop Moderate-Splaining!....101
Climate Inaction in Action....105
The World's Most Extraordinary Income Inequality....110
I'm a Diabetic Afraid of Needles, and I'm Triple-Vaxxed....114

Parents Who Believe in Sexual Purity Should Still Vaccinate Their Kids Against HPV....118
Is There *Anything* I Can Say to Get You to Donate?....122
Do You Smell Smoke?....126
The Cultiest Two Years of My Life....130
Make Christians Christlike Again....139
Let's Celebrate Higher Gas Prices....143
Can We At Least Get a Proxy Apology?....147
Coats When It's Cold, Masks When There's Virus....151
I Scream, You Scream, We All Scream for Pronouns....155
This Isn't the New Normal. These Are the Good Old Days....160
Yes, I'm Offended and I Want to Sin....166
Be a Jerk for Jesus....170
Football Has Fans, Religion Exists, and Climate Change Is Real, Too....176
A Gastric Bypass for Global Warming....181
Ye Cannot Serve Both Love and Hate....187
You Can't Go Home Again, Even If You've Never Left....192
I Give Gays a Bad Name....197
Do Good People Smile Behind Closed Doors When LGBTQ Folks Are Murdered?....205
I'm Spending My Children's Inheritance....210
Acknowledgement of Previous Publication....214
Books by Johnny Townsend....219
What Readers Have Said....231

We Must Adjust to a Changing World

Leaving my suburban American home to work as an LDS missionary in Rome required several lifestyle adjustments.

Years later, when I lost both my job and home in New Orleans to Hurricane Katrina, I was forced to make even more radical adjustments.

Many of us in the LDS community who are white and raised in a white-centric America are now facing an adjustment far more difficult—accepting that, despite our best intentions, we've learned unconscious biases that harm others.

I've always hated math and managed to avoid it completely while earning three English degrees. But then I decided to study biology and discovered I needed trigonometry, physics, and chemistry.

So I adapted.

I still hate math.

But I can do it.

Over the years, I saw friends and coworkers with diabetes and thought I'd rather kill myself than face daily insulin injections. Then I developed diabetes and adapted.

Gradually, my diabetes worsened and I began to need two insulin injections a day.

I adapted again.

Believe me, I still hate needles. But I do what I have to do.

I taught college English for ten years. Then I worked in a public library. Later, I worked as a bank teller. Then I worked as an equity loan processor.

Most of those changes were forced on me by external circumstances. They weren't career goals.

But I adjusted anyway.

In our evolving economy, many of us will face similar career adjustments, even if we stay in the same job.

Maybe our spouse dies or asks for a divorce. Perhaps we're disabled in an accident. Or we're blessed with triplets. Maybe a relative leaves us a sizeable inheritance. The reasons we're forced to adjust in life aren't always within our control.

After relocating to Seattle in the aftermath of Katrina, I was thrilled to find myself in a region where high temperatures in the summer were often in the low to mid-70s.

But I watched as wildfires grew worse every year. Seattle hit an all-time high of 103 in 2009, four years after I moved to the Pacific Northwest. Watching as climate change wreaked havoc in Australia, California, and other areas, I kept hoping we'd escape the worst of it here.

Sure, folks here had adapted to wearing masks, even before the pandemic, to fend off smoke, but it was either that or choke. Still, I was grateful for every day we didn't hit 80 degrees.

Recently, we hit 102. The following day, we hit 104. And the day after that, 108.

We can't pump greenhouse gases into the atmosphere every day and not expect the atmosphere to function as a greenhouse.

We either accept the existence of unintentional biases or we face police killings and nationwide protests and mass incarceration and continual unrest.

Ignoring the reality of structural and institutional racism, hoping it'll miraculously go away on its own or that others will simply stop noticing or complaining is like pumping out more greenhouse gases as a solution for excess greenhouse gases.

Mormons adjusted when we left New York for Pennsylvania. We adjusted again when we moved to Ohio, then Missouri, then Illinois, then Utah.

Most of us adjusted when we went through the temple for the first time and committed to wearing garments for the rest of our lives.

We adjusted when the priesthood and temple ban against Blacks was lifted.

Growing up in the suburbs of New Orleans, I watched as my father put a sledgehammer and an axe in the attic. We might need to chop our way out if we were trapped by rising water.

We're facing a convergence of crises in American life right now, and we must make disruptive adjustments to address them.

We're in a climate crisis. And a healthcare crisis. And a student loan crisis.

We must tear through the roof of structural and institutional racism or drown.

I grew up with fire and tornado drills. Now I practice earthquake and active shooter drills.

Adapting isn't a matter of morality. It's a matter of survival.

And of far more than that—it's a matter of *thriving*, as families, communities, and a nation.

If we want either personal or societal progress, we must accept the necessity of change.

And then—we already know the answer—we need to go ahead and change.

Moral Snobbery, Snarky Comments, and Mockery Rarely Win Converts

We often hear criticism of oppressive political and religious leaders phrased as, "They're on the wrong side of history." It's comforting to know that *we're* right and *they're* wrong.

But it's also true that "History is written by the victors."

When I researched the Upstairs Lounge fire in the late 1980s, I was struck by many inconsistencies. Several articles mentioned "burglar bars" on the windows, but a dozen people escaped through those windows. A coroner's report listed one victim as white when he was a moderately dark-skinned black man. Survivors I spoke with told me other conflicting details.

Ultimately, I had to make sense of the material and construct what seemed to me the most likely version of "reality."

So the question we need to ask about our current political instability is, "Who is going to win the battle between right-wing authoritarianism and human rights?"

The fact that we *want* the answer to be "human rights" doesn't mean it will be.

We're more aware than most that human rights have lost that battle repeatedly throughout history. In the U.S., we've oppressed the indigenous peoples who were here before us, we've oppressed Africans brought over as slaves as well as their descendants. We forced workers into unsafe conditions. We created a Chinese Exclusion Act, interned Americans of Japanese descent. We put LGBTQ folks in prison, denied them housing and jobs.

Even now, we're increasing the size of our homeless population every day.

We have more incarcerated citizens per capita than any other nation on the planet.

We're the only industrialized nation in the world without universal healthcare.

The list of oppressive policies past and present could go on and on.

If we've made some degree of progress over the centuries, that's still no assurance "human rights" will be the ultimate winner in this contest.

On the local level, political operatives driven by power, ideology, or greed are again making it harder for people to vote. A media system creating an alternate reality has already "written" a history that never existed and is predicting a future that will erase what little fact-based narratives still survive.

Recently, a friend in Canada expressed dismay after hearing a news report of the political conditions in the U.S. Despite being relatively aware of the situation, he hadn't realized things were so bad. He asked if the report was exaggerated.

"Did you wake up this morning wondering if your government was going to be overthrown by a coup before the end of the day?" I asked. "We did."

I was once partnered with a man suffering from full-blown AIDS. Every day when I left the apartment, I wondered if he'd still be alive when I returned home that evening.

That's worry on an individual level. Today, I wonder if insurrectionists will storm City Hall or the state legislature or the U.S. Capitol. I wonder if white supremacists embedded in local police departments or the military will begin massive sweeps with no warning.

I *don't* worry about a million men in Confederate uniforms forming a battle line. I worry about bombings and mass shootings. I worry that enough formerly rational people will truly believe I'm an alien lizard who eats babies that they'll show up at my home and murder me or my loved ones.

The fact that I support voting rights, LGBTQ equality, universal healthcare, tuition-free college and vocational training, immediate action on the climate crisis, plus a dozen other sound and humane policies doesn't mean I think those who feel the same will be the ones writing the history books.

Already, textbook content for primary and secondary education is heavily influenced by inaccurate right-wing narratives. What happens when the extreme right gains even more control?

When we say, "History is written by the victors," that's not figurative. It's literal.

Those of us on the left are faced with two huge obstacles: so much of the current narrative is controlled either by extremist right-wing or corporate "centrist" interests that the truth becomes difficult to find.

If workers feel that blacks or immigrants or white people are the problem, they'll fight each other for scraps rather than understand that capitalism is the source of most of our economic and ideological oppression.

Many white people fear they're being replaced and will be oppressed as a result because they've never seen a system where the majority doesn't oppress minorities. We must present a believable case that things can be otherwise.

Those of us on the left face yet another problem—weariness. Folks on the far right are often driven by a religious zeal. We're fighting for the good of humanity (and of the planet) while they're fighting for their very souls.

For them, that's not figurative, either. Many feel their eternal salvation is on the line, so they will "endure to the end" no matter what it costs them personally.

That's an internal fire few on the left can match. Yet it's felt by vast multitudes on their side.

So who's on the right side of history?

We talk a lot about "people power," and it's encouraging to see the rise in worker strikes and other promising developments in the labor movement, but we need to do a much better job at showing those who consistently vote against their own best interests—mostly because they feel *we'll* suffer even more—that there is a way we can all move forward together.

Telling them they're stupid and racist isn't going to cut it.

Moral snobbery, snarky comments, and mockery rarely win converts. Unless we want an actual civil war, we'd better find a more constructive way to deal with the reality that millions of people on the right want us dead.

We may not need to work harder, but we must definitely work smarter to ensure that history books in the coming years prove that racial, social, and economic justice are indeed the right choice.

From Book Burner to Librarian

I hate to admit it, but I'd have burned Mayan books back in the day. I'm ashamed to say I understand the growing hysteria among the far right to ban books from school libraries and to monitor what textbooks their children read.

But while the motivation behind "protecting the children" may stem from a good place, it can only create great harm.

Rather than demonize these parents, though, we need to understand where they're coming from if we want to persuade them to more constructive behavior.

Just as those on the left want to protect their children from learning racist beliefs, from attitudes deeming the disabled as less than, from any harmful ideology, folks on the right also want to protect their children from learning ideas they think are bad.

The problem, of course, is when parents want to keep every other child, indeed every other person of any age, from reading material *they've* decided is inappropriate.

Growing up, I loved monster movies. *Godzilla* was great. *King Kong* was king. *It Came from Outer Space* was a scream. And who didn't love *The Birds* and *The Blob*? "It creeps and leaps and glides and slides across the floor…"

I was raised Christian, with Baptist and Methodist extended family in Mississippi, but my immediate family converted to Mormonism in the suburbs of New Orleans when I was nine. Still, none of this changed my love of monsters.

At twelve, my best friend Jeff and I stayed up late together every weekend watching films like *The Green Slime* and *Five Million Years to Earth* and *Planet of the Apes.* We played board games like *Creature Features* and *Dark Shadows.*

Jeff introduced me to *Famous Monsters of Filmland*, and we both became avid collectors of the magazine. We collected *Creepy* comic magazines. We collected *Eerie* and *Vampirella* and the first issues of *Swamp Thing*.

I even owned a first edition of a novel that was soon to be released as a film. *Star Wars*.

But then I began to feel guilty over my burgeoning sexuality. I was gay and going to hell.

So I decided to throw myself into church meetings and read the Book of Mormon from cover to cover. For better or worse, I became a convert myself. The fact that I was attending a Baptist high school only amplified my religious impulses.

Mormons, for those who don't know, believe there is life on thousands, perhaps millions, of other planets. The tricky part is the belief that intelligent life on those planets is identical to that on Earth—all intelligent life everywhere is human, because we are all made in the image of God, and those good people on Earth who make it to the top of the Celestial Kingdom after death then become gods as well and people their own planets.

With intelligent beings made in our image.

There were no "aliens" on other planets that looked like the creatures in *Star Wars*. There were no werewolves or vampires on Earth or anywhere else. There was no Swamp Thing.

These stories weren't just "fiction," they were *lies.*

Since that was the case, it wasn't good for me to keep these books and magazines. But if they weren't good for me, they weren't good for anyone else, either. Even though I'd loved them for years, and I knew others might, too, it was best they all just go in the trash.

I wasn't going to tell anyone else to throw away their books, of course. Thankfully, I never became that much of a fanatic. I simply didn't feel it ethical to get rid of something I considered bad by polluting someone else's mind. Chucking it all was for my good, it was for their good, it was for everyone's good.

If you were throwing out spoiled potato salad, you wouldn't gift it to your neighbor next door.

I watched from my bedroom window while the trash collectors hauled my rubbish away.

Fortunately, Mormonism also saved me from continuing this destructive behavior.

When I was nineteen, I was "called" to volunteer two years as a missionary in Rome. Living in Italy opened my mind in ways a suburban private school in the States never could. Then when I returned and began pursuing a degree in English, it was impossible to enter the worlds of writers from different centuries and not realize that understanding other people and other cultures was an absolute moral good.

Naturally, along with learning came questioning. And along with questioning came realizing that remaining in a church that hated me was never going to work.

This, of course, is what so many parents rushing to ban books fear. They are fully aware their children might start believing things parents don't want them to believe.

Ideas like "fascism is bad," whether that fascism is practiced by Italians or Germans or even Americans.

Their children might learn that racism isn't simply a particular act or word but operates through a system of laws and policies that favor some people and oppress others, sometimes intentionally and other times through ignorance.

Parents have rights, but so do their children. A handful of parents shouldn't be able to determine what everyone else's children can or can't read. And the rest of us have a right to demand that all citizens we interact with in our communities receive an adequate education. How can we release youth into adulthood after a twelve-year curriculum that affords them little or no in-depth study of racism, sexism, homophobia, genocide, and all the other evils they'll encounter in the "real world"?

That's preparation?

What parent hasn't heard their kids lament, "I'll never need to know trigonometry!"

They *will* need to know about racism, whatever their race.

It's not enough that I can teach my child at home what the schools don't teach. We need all children who will become adult grocers and bankers and attorneys and physicians and politicians to understand this material.

Parents who insist their children live in a bubble must be the ones to take on the responsibility of home schooling, not the other way around. And testing to grant a diploma after that home schooling must still cover this essential material.

I'll admit, I was upset to learn that Christopher Columbus was a brutal man who enslaved indigenous people and cut off their hands as punishment for not bringing him enough gold. I'd been taught in school he was a hero. I'd been taught in church that God had led him to the Americas specifically to ensure that our religion could flourish here.

Sometimes, truths are unpleasant. A cancer diagnosis. The news that our child is a bully. A spouse's indiscretion. But I'd rather know truths and deal with them than live in ignorance. And to have a functioning society, we can't have one set of facts for bubble children and another for the rest.

Every kind of academic change is difficult, whether we're moving from math to algebra, from learning French or Spanish as a second language to learning Latin or Greek or Japanese as a third.

Changing our belief system or our culture is even more difficult. The gay subculture of the French Quarter was nothing like Single Adult socials at church.

Even today, thirty-five years after being excommunicated, I've never had a single alcoholic drink.

Every year, I mark the anniversary of my baptism and the anniversary of the day I entered the Missionary Training Center.

When I lost my job and apartment to Hurricane Katrina and relocated thousands of miles away to the Pacific Northwest, the transition wasn't easy. What constituted "friendliness" in the two cultures was quite different.

I grew up Republican, became a Democrat after coming out, and then moved on to become a Democratic Socialist and finally socialist. Each step along that path was difficult.

Parents naturally don't want their children to choose a different path that might create distance in their relationships.

I lost almost all my friends and family because I read books they'd never dare open, and because I learned something from them.

Some of my ex-Mormon friends burned their personal copies of the Book of Mormon. They encouraged people to shop in thrift stores for old copies of *The Miracle of Forgiveness*, a book filled with hateful doctrine written by one of our former religion's presidents. They encouraged one another to burn every copy they could find.

I'd read that book both in English and Italian, and it was indeed cruel.

But I still had no desire to burn it.

I remembered in one of my college history courses learning that Catholic priests had burned Mayan books, and I'd been horrified, not remembering that I'd done basically the same thing only a few years earlier.

But since then I've read *Maus* and loved it. I read *Lord of the Flies* and *1984* and *Fahrenheit 451.*

No one who has read or understood those books would want to ban them.

I've worked in public libraries in New Orleans and Seattle. I donate materials to archives and special collections, in the U.S. and other countries. I make small donations to independent bookstores.

Some have gloated that *Maus* has become a bestseller after the school library ban. They see this as a victory. But for every book that survives banning, a hundred others are crushed nearly to oblivion.

I'm committed to preservation, not destruction.

I used to believe I was righteous when I threw "lies" away.

No one likes discovering they've been wrong. It's hurtful and embarrassing. It's far easier emotionally to double down.

But as I learned, it's only easier in the short term. Eventually, repression always leads to more repression. If the genuinely worried, loving parents clamoring for more censorship every day had read any of these books, they'd know that.

The good news is that, at least for now, they still can.

I'm My Own Grandchild

Almost every day, we hear climate alarmists shouting, "What kind of world are we leaving our children and grandchildren?"

Frankly, I'm baffled when I hear such appeals. As a climate crisis refugee who lost my job and home to the worst hurricane season on record (since surpassed), who relocated across the country to start my life over at the age of 44, and who has since been forced to wear N95 masks during increasingly severe fire seasons, I don't see the climate emergency as some vague future threat.

If country/western artists can sing "I'm My Own Grandpa," perhaps climate realists can come up with a song of our own—"I'm My Own Grandchild."

A recent incident hardly measures as a blip on our overheated radar. On June 27, 2021, a peaceful Sunday, the town of Lytton in British Columbia recorded Canada's highest temperature ever, 46.6 degrees C. The previous record had been 45, set in 1937 in Saskatchewan. On Monday, Lytton broke the all-time record high it had set the day before, with 47.9. On Tuesday, it broke the all-time record high again, with 49.6 C (over 121 degrees F). On Wednesday, Lytton recorded 49.5 C, just a fraction lower.

That evening, the town of Lytton burned down, 90% of the village wiped out in about fifteen minutes. There's the all-too familiar video taken from residents fleeing by car, flames along both sides of the road, buildings and vehicles ablaze. One survivor didn't have time to get his aging parents into a car, telling them to lie in a ditch and then covering them as best he could.

They didn't survive.

Neither did a billion clams, mussels, and other shellfish, stranded on a blistering hot beach when the tide receded, dead by the time the tide returned.

Year after year, we see raging wildfires across the planet, towns and human lives destroyed, millennia-old sequoias killed, billions of animals wiped out. Fire tornadoes were once so rare that some meteorologists weren't sure they were even real.

What kind of world are we leaving our grandchildren?

What kind of world are we living in *now*?

Many of us recently learned a new term, "wet bulb." Even growing up in New Orleans, oppressed by the heat and humidity, I'd never heard it. In the past, only occasionally would temperature and humidity combine in a way that prevented completely healthy people from regulating their body temperature and dying, without any underlying conditions, even while sitting in the shade.

But those conditions are developing more frequently in more places year after year.

In the terrible heatwaves of 2003 and 2010, when over 100,000 people died across Europe and Russia, the high temperature was mostly in the mid-80s. But because of wet bulb conditions, it was enough to create massive human death.

Did rising sea levels and encroaching salt water contribute to the Surfside condo collapse in Florida that killed 98 people? It's still too early to say in this specific case, but compromised building integrity on a massive scale certainly *will* happen in the coming years.

Climate change doesn't just threaten tiny rural towns anymore. It also threatens the future of Chicago, Venice, Mumbai, and New York. Several years ago, Indonesia began moving its capital from Jakarta to Kalimantan, in part because of climate change. Global warming has brought Lake Mead to its lowest level since its creation, water that's needed to irrigate millions of acres of farmland. And provide drinking water to 25 million people in California, Nevada, Arizona, and Mexico.

Hurricanes, stalling longer and more often because of air currents weakened by climate change, are dropping a year's worth of rain in just a few days on Texas, the Carolinas, and elsewhere. Damage caused by more frequent climate disasters has cost the U.S. over $2 trillion already.

Meanwhile, misuse of groundwater is destroying aquifers around the world, a climate crisis in itself completely apart from greenhouse gases. A global rise in drought is stressing nations across the planet. If we think the current immigration crisis at the U.S. border or throughout Europe is bad now, and it is, hundreds of millions more climate change refugees will soon overwhelm any country left reasonably stable in the midst of increasing disasters.

The unprecedented heat in the Pacific Northwest this year reminds me that even relocating 2600 miles from the last climate disaster I experienced won't spare me. Local crops were destroyed from the heat and trees are dying both from lack of water and because the drought has sparked the release of previously unknown fungi. What was a surprisingly healthy snowpack in February melted away in just a few days, and at least 194 people died in Oregon and Washington, more than three times the number killed when Mt. St. Helens erupted in 1980.

It's not the end of the world, but horrific climate effects aren't a "distant possibility," either.

This also isn't a "new normal" we simply need to get used to. Next year will almost certainly be worse, and the year after that, and each succeeding year, with minor fluctuations unable to mask a clear trend.

We run the risk of "exaggerating" if we say the climate emergency is happening to *us* now. But we run a far greater risk if we keep pretending it's not happening right before our eyes.

The Party That Cried Wolf

"I will cancel student debt immediately," candidate Joe Biden promised.

A year later, he still hasn't delivered, says he "can't."

Again and again, "progressive" members of the Democratic Party promise "access" to healthcare or even Medicare for All. They promise "affordable" education, maybe even tuition-free college and vocational training. They promise subsidized childcare and police reform and "action" on the climate crisis.

And tell us the filibuster prevents them from moving forward with any of it. Blame one or two members of their party for the complete failure of their platform.

They hold the line, stand strong, demand action…and then give in to corporate interests in their party.

The next morning, they start fundraising on their defeat, offer Master classes on their losing strategy, insist that if believers give them just a little more money, they can finally defeat the bad guys keeping them from fulfilling their promises.

A bit like the Whoopi Goldberg character in *Ghost* scamming desperate people wanting one last moment with their dreams.

"I pay more!" one of her marks offers eagerly. "How much?"

But even when Democrats control the White House, the Senate, and the House of Representatives, they willingly approve new fossil fuel projects. They still lock up people at our borders. They show their willingness to "compromise" by giving in again and again. Sometimes, they give in even before they've been asked to.

They'll eliminate gerrymandering…if everyone agrees to play nice.

They'll add more justices to the Supreme Court…maybe…if Republicans agree to give up power.

Whatever the issue, progress is promised and promised. Until it isn't.

"Do as I say, not as I do" is their motto. *We* must give our all to them but they feel no obligation to do the same for us.

Moderate friends of mine grow angry if I suggest the two major parties in the U.S. are the same.

Of *course* they're not the same. Republicans are far more extreme and punitive and destructive.

But after so many decades living with this difference in degree, not substance, we face the choice of being attacked by a lone wolf or a pack. Either way, it's a hard sell for mauled voters.

We may be mauled or even killed by something else if we leave the safety of our herd, but we're desperate enough to try.

Now I'll throw in the requisite Holocaust analogy: trying to escape Sobibor is risky but staying is a death sentence.

The vote *will* be divided. The question is where those votes will go. "Leaders" can promise something their constituents desperately need and then fail to deliver just so many times before no one believes them anymore.

"I promise this is my last drink."

"I promise I'll be completely faithful from now on."

"I promise I'll never hit you again."

Even our friends know the promises are lies. They just feel these are better lies than the other side tells.

To become at least slightly more honest, the Party That Cried Wolf should change its mascot from a donkey to a wolf. A chimera could work, too, a stubborn, lying wolf in sheep's clothing. Pick your losing inspiration.

Rather than join Democrat-Anon to learn how to cope with faithless political leaders, we should instead find a party whose ideals lead naturally to compliance. Stock market investors leading the country clearly have capitalism as their only real constituent.

A people's party, a labor party, a green party, or socialism all have a better chance at addressing our needs. We can disagree on the best options, but what more evidence do we need that Democrats are *not* that option?

Still, I could be wrong. Maybe this time the Party will come through. After all, I did sign another petition yesterday asking Biden to cancel student debt.

He said he'd do it. He said it again and again.

The leader of the Democratic Party wouldn't just *lie*, would he?

Let's Change Our Attitude Toward Race

"Two men looked out from prison bars. One saw mud, the other stars."

"You can eat an elephant if you just eat it a day at a time."

My bishop's wife sent me encouraging quotes about attitude while I was serving as an LDS missionary in Rome. Other friends did, too. Proselytizing in Italy was hard, and these reminders helped.

As Mormons, as conservative Christians, as white people, we need to remind each other that anti-racist work is difficult and that our biggest obstacle is white fragility. But "fragility" is an attitude, and we can improve ours.

Recently, while working in a neighborhood with lots of homeless people, I heard someone knocking on our building's door. As a rule, we kept the front business doors locked and only let in customers by appointment, a COVID precaution that we'd implemented after being shut down for almost a year.

I could see through the glass that this young woman did not have an appointment, but she looked friendly enough, so I buzzed her in. "Can I help you?" I asked.

"We're across the street in the park celebrating Juneteenth," she said. "Is it OK if some of our elderly folks come use your bathroom?"

I'm not particularly good at adapting, but this was an easy call. "Sure," I said. "We're trying to keep the number of people in the building down, but you send any elderly or disabled folks over here, and I'll buzz them in."

A handful of unscheduled folks trickled in throughout the remainder of my shift.

That evening, after I went to bed, I had a difficult time falling asleep, a problem because the following morning, I had a ten-hour shift at a different part-time job, this one requiring a 90-minute commute by public transportation each way.

I needed my beauty sleep.

And my attitude sleep.

By nature, unfortunately, I'm quite irritable, a fault I must work on constantly.

But folks in my neighborhood were shooting off fireworks every ten or fifteen minutes. They'd been doing this a week or so already. An occasional boom here, another boom there. Why people wanted to spend their money on fireworks, especially during a serious drought, was a mystery to me.

And why set off fireworks three weeks before the Fourth of July?

But we were closer now, only two weeks away, and I supposed people simply liked what they liked. The last year and a half had been stressful and folks needed to let off steam.

The booms continued, and then grew louder, and multiplied in number. Boom, boom, boom! I hoped our dry lawn didn't catch fire. BOOM, BOOM, BOOM! Sheesh, they were going to break a window. Twenty more minutes. Thirty. Forty-five.

What in the world was going on? Did people not have calendars?

Finally, of course, despite my late-night stupor, I figured it out. My neighbors were celebrating Juneteenth.

The instant I understood the reason for the disturbance, my attitude changed. What a wonderful new annoyance to experience every year, I realized.

I wondered if in past years, some of the "pre-Fourth of July" fireworks I'd heard were set off for the same reason.

While I was struggling as a door-to-door salesman trying to sell Mormonism to Catholics in Rome, my bishop's wife sent me another encouraging note, a short anecdote about the life of a woman who'd been forced to relocate from the East Coast to the desert in Arizona. She was terribly unhappy, miserable.

Until she noticed a tiny plant she'd never seen before. She started noticing other interesting vegetation, even out in this "desolate" area, and kept studying. Eventually, she became such an expert that she wrote a book on the flora of the Southwest.

It was all in the attitude, the bishop's wife reminded me.

So I worked on improving my poor attitude once again.

I eventually left Mormonism, but I kept most of the good things I learned about Italian life and culture. My husband is also an ex-Mormon who "served" his mission in Italy. Forty years later, we watch Italian shows and movies all the time. We know how to make a good lasagna. I still listen to Italian pop.

If you haven't seen the music video for Laura Pausini's "Io sì," take a look.

Italy has problems, but there's much to celebrate. Mormonism has problems, but my husband and I still keep part of its culture in our lives.

America, as we know, has a multitude of problems, but there is also much to celebrate here.

And one of those causes for celebration is Juneteenth, commemorating the end of slavery. That's something even fragile white people should be able to get behind.

Trying to repair even a few of the many wrongs our nation has perpetrated against its own people or others around the world is daunting. It will make us irritable, even if that's not our usual state.

But most of the annoyance, and much of the weariness, can be alleviated if we just muster up a better attitude.

We can look at the state of our nation and see mud.

With only a slight change of attitude, though, we can see stars.

Student Loans Create Chronic Stress

There's been a lot of talk lately about canceling student loan debt. Perhaps $10,000 of it. Maybe up to $50,000.

Who knows?

But there sure is a lot of talk. And talk. And talk. And talk.

Meanwhile, I've been paying my student loan consistently ever since I graduated. I was three days late once and had my interest rate raised by a full point as a result, but the rest of the time, I've managed to pay on schedule.

Not that there haven't been a few distractions along the way.

You know, like 9/11.

And the U.S. going to war with Iraq and Afghanistan.

And my husband dying of liver cancer.

A devastating tsunami in the Indian Ocean.

Losing my job and apartment to Hurricane Katrina.

Moving across the country to start over with just a single suitcase. (Full disclosure—I did get a six-month reprieve from payments during this time).

Then there was finding a job at a payday loan center.

And being forced to relocate again when my apartment building was torn down.

There was the thrill of a new job at a credit union.

Until my branch closed.

There was the stress of moving from temp job to temp job. (It was during this period I was three days late for a payment.)

I found steady employment again.

I remarried.

A damaged nuclear reactor in Japan sent radiation around the world. The Arab Spring erupted across North Africa. MH370 disappeared without a trace. Occupy Wall Street came and went.

A meteor exploded over Siberia.

The residents of Flint, Michigan, were poisoned.

My grandmother died. And my father.

And, since I'm getting older, a few friends died, too. Like Jim, and Nicla, and William, and Tim, and Alan, and Richard.

And Burt, who was murdered.

There were some good times, too, of course. Like the entire 12-year run of *The Big Bang Theory.* All the Harry Potter movies.

Two terms of the first African-American president.

The Me Too movement.

Greta Thunberg.

And there yet were still more distractions.

You know, like Beirut blowing up. And wildfires destroying entire towns in the U.S. and Canada. And a global pandemic.

The Black Lives Matter movement.

An insurrection.

Jeff Bezos rocketing into space.

Widespread medical problems from chronic stress.

Every day, there's something. People fleeing a Greek island by ferry, surrounded by flames. Desperate Afghans clinging to the wheels of a plane taking off. A condo collapsing in Florida. An earthquake in Haiti. Floods in Belgium and Germany. In Tennessee. In New York.

Anti-maskers threatening to kill people.

You know…life.

The years roll on, millions of people dying, millions more being born, the Earth rushing closer and closer to a greenhouse gas tipping point from which it cannot recover even in the lifetimes of those who will be born years from now on the day I make my last student loan payment.

It doesn't have to be this way. We've made a choice to crush students with debt. Other countries have made better choices.

We're free to change our minds and make better choices, too.

While we strive to make lives better, we're faced with hundreds of distractions every day, year after year. But we must keep our minds focused on the essentials.

We need tuition-free college and vocational training. An educated, trained population not crushed by debt is the only way we can hope to stay competitive in a global economy…or be truly free in our own country.

We need universal healthcare. A healthy population not crushed by debt also leads to innovation and stability.

And a massive, all-out effort to move away from fossil fuels as we adapt to climate change is the only way any of us will even have the luxury of worrying about student loans. Or education at all.

But I'm getting distracted again.

In five days, my next student loan payment is due. Thank God I get my paycheck the day before.

Every Newscast Must Discuss Climate

As David Sirota pointed out in a recent interview on MSNBC, an occasional mention of climate change isn't enough to reflect the seriousness of the crisis. We need discussion of climate in every single newscast.

When I visited my grandparents as a child, I was fascinated by their obsession with the weather. They only received two stations in rural Mississippi, both a bit fuzzy. They'd tune in first to Channel 3, which delivered the weather forecast at 6:18. Then they'd switch to Channel 12, which delivered the forecast at 6:23.

My grandparents were farmers and wanted to be doubly sure they knew what to expect in the coming hours.

Another early memory is wondering why so much airtime was wasted on sports. There was a war in Vietnam, Watergate trials in Washington, long lines at the gas station. And we needed to spend a full quarter of every newscast on games?

Of course, sports was followed by millions and brought in hundreds of millions of dollars. It was "newsworthy."

Until climate catastrophe and the world's sixth mass extinction event are treated as comparable to the latest basketball game, we have no hope of adapting to the changes we're already facing.

Wildfires burn entire towns, increasingly severe storms and more frequent flooding events cost more and more each year.

When my grandparents watched two weather forecasts, it was for confirmation or to understand slight variations. It wasn't to get "both sides" on the coming hailstorm or overnight freeze. They didn't see one forecast for a 10% chance of rain and another for a 90% chance and then decide which forecast they were going to believe before deciding whether or not to bale hay. All forecasts were based on the best science available at the time.

Of course, given the facts, it might be depressing to spend five minutes of every newscast on climate. And climate news could be scary.

As if news about rising fascism and the decline of our democracy isn't?

Would a news anchor start her broadcast with, "Ten homes in the northeast part of the city collapsed into a sinkhole this afternoon. We'll be bringing you a special report next week at 11:00"?

Crises are newsworthy *right now.*

Ongoing crises like the embassy takeover in Tehran or the Great Recession or the pandemic get covered in every single newscast.

Greta Thunberg points out that we need to treat the climate crisis as if our house is on fire.

If corporations and the wealthy control politicians, and politicians control policy, then the only way to create change is to show people the importance of climate by setting aside part of every newscast, local and national, to cover the crisis.

Of course, since all major news networks are corporate themselves, and since they receive ad revenue from fossil fuel corporations, we must pressure the networks.

But we can't just wait for them to do their job. And we can't just complain when they don't do it. The job needs to be done, and while we pressure, we must simply do the job ourselves as best we can.

Whether we're making movies about climate to force the conversation, or writing books, holding rallies, boycotting, speaking with our elected officials, commenting publicly in city council meetings, or whatever else our circumstances allow, we must include climate in everything we do.

Sending a winter holiday card featuring a snowy landscape to friends and family? Include a note about rising global temperatures. Sending congratulations to a loved one on the birth of their child? Include a note expressing your sincere wish that society takes the climate crisis seriously so that the child will have a habitable world to live in.

I buy blank greeting cards with photos of fossils or paintings of dinosaurs for just this purpose.

Am I a sick fuck?

Perhaps, but to paraphrase Jennifer Lawrence's character in *Don't Look Up*, "We're all gonna die!"

My country-raised mom shouted this every time we merged onto the freeway, so it comes naturally to me.

We can be kind, and funny, and friendly, *and* insist that climate is important enough to include in every conversation.

When a coworker mentioned cities where she might like to relocate in five years, I said, "Oh, those are great choices. But do remember that the Thwaites glacier will probably have melted by then and that sea levels may have risen a meter. And don't forget which areas seem most likely to be hit with expanding desertification or heavier rainfalls."

Am I a killjoy?

Is covering the pandemic in newscasts a buzzkill?

The answer may well be yes in both cases, but just because we don't *want* to talk about these things doesn't mean we don't need to.

If society is going to mobilize enough to address the climate crisis in any meaningful way, the topic must be important enough to speak about for at least five minutes in each newscast. And until that happens, it's up to us to keep it in the minds of our friends, families, and coworkers.

And in our own minds.

We all need to escape once in a while, and we all need a balanced life in order to sustain mental health.

But denial as our primary strategy isn't healthy. That's true when the issue is disease or fascism or corporate influence or climate disaster.

And if we can't make mainstream news cover the climate adequately, let's stop supporting them and instead support independent news that does cover the stories we need to hear.

Second Thought: An Introductory Socialist YouTube Channel to Share with Friends and Family

Second Thought is a socialist YouTube channel with 1.4 million subscribers offering bite-sized lessons ranging from ten to twenty minutes, addressing one topic at a time. It's perfect for those just learning about socialism who lack the time or motivation to read academic political theory or attend a community forum but who might enjoy a single video on a topic they care about.

Even those of us able to dedicate a bit more time to study sometimes find it easier to watch a mini-lesson than read a dense article. And the videos offer consistently good content we can insert as hyperlinks in articles and commentaries of our own.

The simplicity of the content also helps veteran socialists who aren't comfortable coming up with quick answers while being interviewed by reporters at protests. Each video delivers one or two succinct points on a relevant topic.

The host has a quirky sense of humor that comes across as nerdy without being cringeworthy. In one video, he explains how capitalism incentivizes food waste over feeding the poor. In another, how the internet could only be created because profit wasn't the underlying motive. He might show how Democrats fund the far right, ask whether or not retirement is still feasible, or explain why billionaire philanthropy cannot solve problems created by the system that also created those billionaires.

One practical video shows viewers how to create socialist content on our own channels—what kind of mic to get, how to find useful royalty-free video clips, what to worry about when taping and what not to worry about.

Some titles include "Socialism for Absolute Beginners," "Is Capitalism Actually Efficient?" "Does Capitalism Really Drive Innovation?" "Do Socialists Just Want to Take Your Stuff?" "Are You Really 'Free' Under Capitalism?" "How Capitalism Exploits Natural Disasters," "The Importance of Revolutionary Optimism," and "You're Probably Already a Socialist."

The host debunks common myths about socialism most of us have grown up accepting as fact. And he just as successfully debunks fabricated "truths" we've been taught that bolster an unwarranted faith in capitalism, important because many Americans have been indoctrinated to believe capitalism is divine. There's even a video explaining how conservative Christianity was co-opted to make questioning capitalism downright heresy.

We can also watch videos about "How 'Moderates' Serve the Right," "How Corporations Shifted the Blame for Climate Change," "Why American Healthcare Is the Worst in the Developed World," "How Capitalism

Destroys Radical Movements," "Are Landlords Really That Bad?" "Astroturfing: How to Spot a Fake Movement," and "Is This the Beginning of a New Labor Movement?"

Second Thought has well over a hundred videos, so it's simple to find a topic we can share with folks able to get past that demonized word "socialist." The titles pose questions even those most vulnerable to the current red scare have asked themselves.

There's "Why Is Everything Turning into Uber?" "The Minimum Wage Debate Explained," "How Feel Good Stories Let a Broken System Off the Hook," "America's Overwork Obsession," "How Finland Ended Homelessness," "The Electoral College Is Anti-Democracy," "How Hollywood Sells Us War," and "This Is How Long It Would Take You to Earn a Billion Dollars."

The well-produced playlist goes on and on.

Even if we're fully versed on most of these topics, they're handy refreshers when something is back in the news and we want persuasive points ready to bring up in friendly discussions with those still misled by corporate propaganda.

These videos pushed me personally to move on from Democratic Socialism to the understanding that only by eliminating capitalism altogether do we as a society and as a species have any real shot at survival. If we have loved ones who aren't quite convinced yet, a few of these videos from *Second Thought* are definitely worth a friendly share.

Weekend and Holiday Transit Schedules Hurt the Most Vulnerable Riders

"Good news! You get to work the holiday! Time and a half for you!"

Yes, that *almost* brings my income up to a living wage—I spend a full 50% on housing—but the news still leaves me feeling like shit.

The poorest people, the most desperate, those without seniority, those who must accept any job offered, those working second and third jobs, are those who work weekends, holidays, late nights, and graveyard shifts.

We're the ones who ride two, three, sometimes four buses to reach our job site and another two, three, or four to return home.

We're the ones whose commute jumps from 90 minutes to 2 hours and 15 minutes when buses switch to their weekend and holiday schedule.

It almost feels like a deliberate attempt to make the most miserable people even more miserable. Because it *is* deliberate. Tax codes don't evolve naturally out of the primordial slime.

I lost one job because the shift ended at midnight and the last bus out of the neighborhood departed at 11:07.

I needed three buses to reach another job, except on Sundays. On Sundays, I only needed two buses.

Why? Because one of the buses I usually rode didn't run on Sunday mornings.

I had to leave the house at 5:45 a.m., walk fifteen minutes in the dark, often in the cold and rain, to reach what was normally my first transfer point. Then I caught the second bus at 6:05, reaching the next transfer point at 6:25. The third bus didn't arrive until 6:45, so I waited in the dark in a "bad" part of town for twenty minutes until it showed up.

I couldn't simply choose to arrive later than 6:25 because the next arrival of the bus that brought me was 6:55. The miserable wait was unavoidable.

After boarding the last bus of the commute, I arrived at my final stop around 7:05. Now I only had to walk three blocks down darkened streets, stepping over homeless people asleep on the sidewalk, to reach my job site. One hour and twenty-five minutes after leaving my home. All within city limits, and not even halfway across the city.

At the last Public Transit Advisory Board meeting I attended, I listened as one of the board members boasted that because of their efforts, any resident in the city could arrive at work within forty minutes.

This was a well-meaning board member, volunteering his time. It was just that he and some of the other board members, while strong advocates for public transit, only rode when doing so was convenient. At other times, they drove their cars.

People with options have the privilege to see things through windshield-colored glasses.

"Lightly traveled" routes are routinely sacrificed, even during weekdays. Those of us who use them during "off peak" days, of course, are deemed even less deserving, possessing only part-time humanity.

Riders fortunate enough to be housed are grateful. Riders fortunate to have jobs are grateful, too. But we still resent that the rich who refuse to pay their fair share *depend* on our gratefulness, depend on our fear of losing everything, to keep us quiet and thankful for the scraps thrown our way.

"Bus drivers need vacations, too, you know. They want to relax with their friends and family, too."

We get it. But "the public" still has needs. We know because *we* still have to serve them. Grocery stores are open. Hospitals are open. And our workplaces are clearly open as well.

"There's not enough money in the city or county budget to keep buses running all the time."

Oh, we're quite aware of that, too.

Every day, we hear in countless ways that we're just so much shit to be tolerated, part of the sewage system infrastructure to keep the houses of the lightly taxed smelling fresh and clean. Sub-human Morlocks serving the Eloi. Whether or not we're "educated" enough to get the reference, we sure do get the message.

Really, though, most of us are okay with working weekends and holidays. We're not asking to sit under beach umbrellas eating bonbons. We just don't want lawmakers and those who lobby them making our commutes any harder than they already are.

In a world facing an increasingly desperate climate crisis, we must invest heavily in public transit and high-speed rail, phasing out fossil fuels far more quickly than any current proposal. But aside from greenhouse gases, equity is also at stake. As Gustavo Petro, former mayor of Bogotá, once pointed out, a "developed country" isn't one where more poor people own cars but one where rich people ride public transportation.

Weekend and holiday transit schedules may not be our top priority—universal healthcare and tuition-free college and vocational training certainly rank higher—but if it takes a three- or four-hour round trip to access any of that, public transit is not a separate, isolated issue.

The wealthiest 5% of our fellow citizens—wealthy because *we* come in to work for them on regular workdays, weekends, and holidays—expect us to be grateful to wade through their sewers because it beats not being incinerated outright in a waste facility. But we aren't, in fact, "happy as a pig in shit."

We're as unhappy as people in shit.

We all know that freedom isn't free. Equity isn't free, either. Neither is a sustainable climate.

It's not that we "want" these things or feel "entitled" to them. We *need* them to have a functioning society and avoid the collapse of civilization.

Advocates and allies must do more than look on the bright side. We must demand funds from the only source that can provide them—corporations and wealthy individuals who, even in the midst of all this need, aren't being asked to do anything more than simply pay their fair share.

Pro-Corporate Programming as 'Feel Good' Drama

I fell in love with the Vespa when I lived in Italy 40 years ago. My two years there left me with many great memories, but one was certainly the ubiquitous little scooter zipping through traffic everywhere I went.

So when the television movie *Enrico Piaggio: Vespa* aired, about the creator of the scooter and his struggles to develop it, I simply had to watch. I was fascinated to learn the Vespa almost disappeared from Italian life by the early 1950s, until Piaggio made the pivotal decision to interest director William Wyler to feature it in his film *Roman Holiday*.

Who among us—of a certain age—can't instantly recall images of Audrey Hepburn and Gregory Peck zipping around Rome on that Vespa? It was a historic success for product placement.

And that's where I started to go sour on the Enrico Piaggio movie. The overwhelming presence of corporate power is the real protagonist of the story. And is clearly victorious.

The movie jumps back and forth between 1952, when *Roman Holiday* was being filmed, and the early years immediately after WWII. Piaggio is "ruined" when his airplane factory is bombed. He can't rebuild because once the war is over, there's no further need for his planes. He must do something else.

So he decides to make a scooter.

Piaggio has difficulty getting a loan for a variety of reasons but does finally succeed in rebuilding. All goes well until the creditor demands repayment. Piaggio is almost destroyed again but then saves the day by…selling one of his Rafael paintings.

It's not that Enrico Piaggio didn't face obstacles, and it's not that he didn't create a great product. It's the framing that's the issue. He was able to do these things because even after a devastating war he still had enough capital to ensure himself options. He had resources that others didn't have.

And the film depicts him as superior because of his achievements. While he may have accomplished something that others with the same resources didn't, the fact remains that he didn't do it from sheer strength of character. He did it because he was raised in a rich, privileged family, was given a strong education because of his privilege, was given management experience because his father owned the factory before him, and still had enormous resources even after his country was devastated by war.

That difference isn't trivial.

Piaggio makes several disparaging comments about "communists" and "union workers," and the implication is he could have achieved much more if he didn't have to deal with such petty grievances. When things are at their lowest and his unpaid workers take over the factory, Piaggio is distressed the workers don't have more faith in him. If those small-minded people could just be patient and give him a little more time, they'd be fine. It's clearly a heavy burden to deal with such short-sighted humans.

Piaggio's depicted as a hero of the working class because he hired these workers in the economic aftermath of the war so he could build his Vespa, which of course brought Piaggio far more money than it ever brought any of his workers, however nice their union pay might have been.

There's also no real discussion that part of Piaggio's wealth came from building warplanes for the bad guys. You know, Mussolini and Hitler. Remember them?

All this isn't to say that Piaggio was a villain. According to the film, he took a bullet to prevent the Germans from taking his workers to Germany against their will. Of course, one can't help wondering if even then he wasn't thinking more about himself. After all, the loss of those workers would directly affect his own income. Regardless, the heroic act itself, according to the film, consisted of little more than smoking a cigarette.

We also watch Piaggio nobly give up other women in order to marry a war widow. A rich war widow, of course, but the important thing is he sacrificed sexual freedom to marry her.

Yeah, I guess that makes him a good guy.

We also see him give a kitten to the widow's daughter while he's courting the woman. The movie consistently gives us these simplistic, uncomplicated visions of good and evil, attempting to manipulate the viewer. Piaggio's so good, according to this account, he could probably be canonized.

It's this lack of complexity that makes the pro-corporate writing throughout the film so irritating. It's a "feel good" drama showing that no matter how bad things might get, corporations and capitalism are always there to save the day.

Day after day, year after year, as I watch capitalism destroy the world, I need a more complex storyline in the films I watch, even when they praise a fossil fuel-using product I actually do like, made famous by an Audrey Hepburn movie I all out adore.

Will Capitalism Reign During the Millennium?

I can't wait for the Millennium when we all work six days a week, twelve or fourteen or even sixteen hours a day. I can't wait for that serene society, when Satan has been bound and we can send our six-year-old children to work in the mines or shuck oysters from dawn until dusk. I can't wait for this future without war, when there are also no workplace safety rules.

That will be heaven on Earth, a thousand years of peace and happiness.

Growing up as a member of The Church of Jesus Christ of Latter-day Saints, I dreamed often about the Millennium. Many of the teens in my congregation received Patriarchal Blessings predicting they'd live to see the Second Coming of Jesus Christ.

As a bullied kid who'd memorized Helen Reddy's "Leave Me Alone," I could only hope that day came sooner rather than later.

In my sixties now, I've long since understood that if the world is going to become a better place, it's up to us to make it happen. Many conservative Christians complain that "kids today" or "sinners" or "Democrats" refuse to take responsibility for their actions while at the same time, we shrug our shoulders, waiting for someone else to solve the problems *we've* helped create.

For many conservatives, religion has become fused with both politics and economics. We believe that capitalism, a system which postdates the Bible and the events of the Book of Mormon by many centuries, is the only righteous form of economics. We simultaneously believe that the love of money is the root of all evil and that the poor live in poverty because they are sinful, lazy, and undeserving.

We believe fathers should be breadwinners while mothers stay home with the kids. Yet there is almost no city in the entire country where a family can rent a one-bedroom apartment on a full-time minimum wage income. How many kids do we expect loving parents to squeeze onto their own mattress?

Yet when workers demand a living wage, we call them slackers who just want free money.

A school district near San Francisco recently issued a call to parents to house their children's teachers because those teachers are leaving the area, no longer able to afford either rent or a mortgage. Such a solution assumes, of course, that teachers are single and will remain so, or that the teacher's entire family will live in that one rented room.

Is our economic system so righteous it can't be tweaked even a little?

Unfettered capitalism gave us the Triangle Shirtwaist Factory fire. It's given us building and bridge collapses, the opioid epidemic, even nuclear accidents. It's given us political leaders bought by wealthy donors.

We now have 40-hour work weeks. We have paid vacation, a minimum wage, child labor laws, and much more. Business owners didn't grant those out of the goodness of their hearts. They were forced to do it through strikes, boycotts, and eventually legislation.

"It's wrong to force people to be good!" I've heard my former missionary companions say.

We have laws forcing companies not to sell food with cheap, dangerous ingredients. We have laws punishing those who steal cars from our driveways. So why is it sinful to have laws preventing employers from stealing wages from their employees?

During the Millennium, I suppose, we'll no longer need regulations. Bosses will simply *choose* to be good to their employees.

But if treating employees fairly is the right thing to do during the Millennium, why do we celebrate *not* treating employees fairly now?

We cheer Howard Schultz as he closes Starbucks locations that have voted to unionize. We admire Jeff Bezos for being savvy enough to destroy small businesses. We applaud executives at UPS for removing air conditioners from their trucks so that delivery drivers don't dawdle in comfort.

Would we accept a thief stealing our TV now because in the Millennium, no one will steal from us?

Why, then, do we accept an economic system designed to concentrate wealth into the hands of a few, a system based on the concept that basic housing and clean water are reserved only for adherents of the prosperity gospel?

Is it heresy to speak against an economic system never once championed by Moses, Nephi, or Jesus?

Profit has become an idol that many conservative Christians worship, sacrificing kindness, dignity, and mercy on the altar to appease it.

We can't alleviate suffering and act humanely until we recognize the obstacles impeding us.

Imperfect humans can never create a heaven on Earth. But we can certainly do better than make life hell for millions.

We can start by accepting that capitalism is not synonymous with faithfulness. We don't need to profit at the expense of others to be worthy of our spot in the Millennium.

So let's separate religion from politics and economics. It's the least we can do to prepare for the thousand years of peace we want.

Homeless Sweeps and Seattle's Lack of Compassion

"Compassion Seattle" is just the latest attack in yet another city on the most vulnerable members of our society. It's a charter amendment that permanently encodes actions like sweeps so that neither voters nor the city council can stop them. According to House Our Neighbors, the charter amendment is backed by private donors and PACs that are pro-developer, many of the same individuals mounting a Recall Sawant campaign to remove a bold socialist already elected three times to the city council.

Around the country, and indeed around the world, corporate interests fund proposals that sometimes *sound* good on the surface but instead make things worse. If the word "Compassion" is in the name, after all, it can't be bad. Plus, Charter Amendment 29 in Seattle will require that 12% of the City's general fund go toward "human services and homeless programs and services," mostly by relocating people into "emergency" housing and constructing 2000 units of "affordable" housing within a year.

It's *something*, right? A "start."

Of course, at last count, back in January of 2020, before the pandemic hit and homelessness skyrocketed in Seattle, there were already over 11,750 homeless people living on the streets here.

And 11% of the budget already goes to human services and homeless programs, so we're agreeing to the bad parts of the amendment just to get a few extra dollars, almost none of it going to those who need it most. Homeless people are *already* living in emergency housing—tents, boxes, doorways, whatever they can manage. And affordable housing isn't the same for someone making $65,000 a year as it is for unemployed and low-wage workers.

Nowhere in the U.S. can someone working a full-time, minimum wage job afford to rent a two-bedroom apartment. In 93% of U.S. counties, a full-time, minimum wage worker can't even afford a one-bedroom apartment. For those unable to work, a monthly disability check often provides less than a minimum wage job. And even disabled folks who are employed can legally be paid less than the minimum wage.

When the police, assisted by the Parks department, conduct sweeps of homeless encampments, employed but unhoused folks trying to get back on their feet must coordinate moving their belongings with still arriving at work on time. Sometimes, volunteers help relocate homeless folks with their belongings before a sweep, and then the sweep simply targets the new location instead.

Poverty pimps—organizations that "serve" homeless populations—make their living seeking grants to "help." Since we have no way to ensure that these jobs have a limited lifespan, administrators have a vested interest in *not* solving the problem. They'd be out of a job.

That's not to say everyone working with one of these organizations is actively sabotaging viable solutions. But even when dedicated humanitarians get grants and donations to provide sleeping bags and other items for homeless folks, the police and Parks employees follow that success by conducting sweeps and throwing all of that investment into the trash. The organizations then seek grants and donations to supply new sleeping bags, and the whole, horrible cycle continues.

During these sweeps, it's not just dirty sleeping bags that are confiscated, of course. People lose their IDs as well, making it virtually impossible to apply for a job or even assistance.

Sweeping a neighborhood "clean" of homeless encampments doesn't solve the problem in any event. It just transfers problematic human beings temporarily. The homeless are worse off, having lost what few possessions they have, and the "community" in the new area where the homeless people have been forced to relocate are now the ones enduring the tents and garbage and needles. All that money and effort, yet we do nothing constructive to solve the problem.

Making miserable people more miserable doesn't provide job skills or rehab or mental health therapy or anything else that helps. It certainly doesn't provide bootstraps.

Even housed residents in the newly cleaned neighborhoods can't enjoy their relief for long. Homeless people set up encampments there to begin with because these neighborhoods are close to the necessities which keep them alive.

They'll be back because the problems that pushed them there haven't been resolved.

How many times have *we* faced a problem but put it off because we were too busy or too stressed to deal with it right at that moment? People struggling to eat healthy food but with no access to refrigeration don't have the capacity to solve the complex problems that led to their homelessness.

The long game with sweeps and other types of "tough love" policies is to find permanent housing. But how long a game are we talking? And where do we expect these people to live in the meantime? Do we expect them to stop having bodily functions for that entire time?

Six years to house 12,000 homeless people. That's a long time to cross your legs and clench.

At best, most cities and counties in the U.S. make an attempt at half measures. We provide clean needles but then don't pick up the dirty needles. We provide trash receptacles but then don't empty them. And we make sure that housed residents and small business owners see the trash and danger in the hope they'll resent both homeless people and any help offered them.

But it doesn't need to be this way. In the U.S., Columbus, Houston, and Salt Lake City have reduced their homeless populations in healthier ways. Vienna, Austria has also seen some success.

A spokesperson for Finland's Housing First program found that while it's enormously expensive to house homeless folks, the country still spends €15,000 *less* per individual homeless person than it costs to leave them on the streets.

So it's not that we don't have the money to house our homeless people, provide job training, and medical and psychological treatment for conditions that have contributed to their desperation. We already spend far more on *not* housing our neighbors.

Acting humanely is a matter of will. And of common sense.

Because even with the most selfish of motives, it's still in *our* best interest to develop policies that reduce homelessness. We must stop letting monied forces trick us into maintaining the status quo—or even worsening conditions—just to allow policy makers to keep wealth at the top.

Disdain for the Deluded

When I hear Mike Lindell and other Trump followers claim, again and again, that they have "proof" Trump won the election and that all will be revealed "soon," I experience flashbacks to my years as a devout Mormon.

Joseph Smith, our founding prophet, assured us that if we truly understood how wonderful even the lowest degree of heaven was, we'd all kill ourselves to get there. If he knew such details, clearly the Mormon version of a tiered heaven was real. He had inside information.

Latter-day Saints have long been promised that "soon," there will be so much archeological evidence proving the Book of Mormon is true that everyone around the world will be forced to acknowledge it. If we have any lingering doubts ourselves, we can relax and dismiss them. We "know" that evidence is coming, and that's good enough.

Again and again, we're told what to believe, told we're supposed to question, but then if we do question and come up with a different answer, we're labeled as faithless or deceived. We're accused of "listening to the wrong spirit."

We see ourselves as open-minded, but only if we all believe the same thing.

After I was excommunicated, my apostasy was announced publicly twice, once to the stake-wide Single Adult organization over which I volunteered as co-chair and again to my home congregation. Everyone needed to be alerted to the danger I posed.

I felt like Veronica Cartwright at the conclusion of *Invasion of the Body Snatchers*.

Most of the friends I'd known for years refused to talk to me, would see me and cross the chapel to avoid me. Those who did talk to me called me a traitor, a Judas, a son of perdition.

Those who managed not to despise me instead cried over me. They prayed for me. They sent my name to the temple so those in the prayer circle there could pray for me as well.

And they let me know all this to show how much they "cared."

While all that hatred and condescending pity helped me escape a tremendously oppressive mindset and culture, I don't want to repeat that patronizing behavior and say the same thing in return, either about believing Mormons or about Trump worshippers.

We were all essentially suffering from Stockholm Syndrome. We were Patty Hearst forced to aim weapons at bank employees, Patty forgetting she could run away when she was finally left alone for the first time after a year and a half of captivity.

Even so, it's impossible not to laugh about Uncle Jerry who believes Democrats are cannibals or our coworker who believes in Jewish space lasers. It's irresistible not to make fun of the ridiculous.

Injecting bleach. Really?

Still, it's one thing to ridicule those at the top setting the delusional agenda, and another to sneer at the lowly followers who "know not what they do."

As Mormons, we were only allowed to do "research" using LDS-approved sources, so most of us remained deceived. If we doubted, our teachers and bishops and other leaders would tell us, "I had a personal revelation and know beyond a shadow of a doubt the Church is true. Rely on my testimony until you have one of your own."

It's not easy for conservative Trump believers to escape a huge framework of lies. They'll hate being described as ensnared or cultish or the other negative ways the rest of us view them.

Everyone likes to see themselves as superior. We're better because *we* didn't "fall away from the gospel." Or we're better because *we* "saw through the lies."

But I identify with the deluded. I identify with those who break free.

I identify with the frustrated. And I identify with the hopeful.

Moral one-upmanship may feel satisfying, but it's not constructive.

Those of us who have escaped soul-crushing mindsets will fare better emotionally and have a stronger chance at persuading at least a few others still trapped if we view those delusional friends, families, and neighbors as human beings oppressed by the same liars and gaslighters who oppress us.

A longtime friend of mine suffering from schizophrenia was plagued for decades with auditory hallucinations. When she was finally diagnosed and started receiving treatment, she called me, distraught.

"Now that I'm on anti-delusional medication," she wailed, "I no longer believe in God!"

Like a spouse who knows their significant other is cheating on them but can pretend it isn't true as long as the words aren't spoken out loud, many on the right feel more comfortable accepting what they already suspect are lies.

It's hard to leave a culture you've known perhaps all your life and realize you'll be hated by those you love. We're expecting people to accept being attacked as "fair game," risk various emotional and actual fatwas against them.

Finding another community after I left Mormonism wasn't easy. Some in the gay sub-culture I entered were afraid of me because of my background. Or disdainful. Even my eventual husband, another ex-Mormon, confided that after our first date, he told himself he'd never get involved with someone who had such a problematic history.

We got out, though, we tell ourselves. If we can be strong and brave and risk everything, so can these other deluded folks.

It's true that some of these religious and political extremists so thoroughly relish being awful to others that whatever culpability they may or may not possess on a cosmic level, it's not safe for us to be around them. If they're redeemable, it will only be after backbreaking effort, and we are not responsible to do their hard work for them.

I'm reminded of a classmate in a graduate program who wore neo-Nazi T-shirts to class, when everyone else in the class was either Jewish, Black, female, gay, or a combination thereof.

We're hardly behaving much better when we use dismissive, even vicious behavior against our deluded right-wing friends and relatives. That behavior doesn't miraculously become honorable when moderate Democrats attack those further to the left who are demanding more action on climate and healthcare and other social justice issues. And when those of us on the far left see moderates as still deluded and treat them as mortal enemies, we're violating one of our most essential principles—solidarity is a healthier strategy than divide and conquer.

I didn't like shunning, hate, and disdain when it came from the deluded, and I don't like it any better from the enlightened.

Insulting millions of Trump supporters, or millions of corporate Democrats, or millions of social justice advocates isn't going to solve our problems any more than Bill Maher's fat shaming will cure obesity.

I don't know "the answer," of course. But disdain isn't it. Whoever does come up with an approach that both tampers down the brewing civil unrest in our nation and creates some willingness to cooperate will probably be awarded the Nobel Peace Prize.

But even if we're not brilliant enough to be that great leader, let's at least try to come up with humane ways to reconnect with the humanity in those who may never try to do it themselves unless we take that step first.

COVID Analogies Are the New Holocaust Analogies

Holocaust analogies are almost always problematic, either because of their inaccuracy (think MTG) or their inherent offensiveness. I must admit, though, one such analogy keeps creeping back into the secret annex of my brain every time I turn on the news.

I watch GOP officials and conservative religious leaders denounce vaccines, as they label masks child abuse. I listen to the nonsensical misinformation about human magnetism and second-hand infertility. I grapple with the logic of claiming the virus is a biological weapon sent by China and then thinking it's patriotic to willingly die from infection without attempting to save ourselves.

And I wonder if it would even be possible to design a more effective method of spreading a fatal disease.

I feel I'm watching millions of people giddily, proudly, obliviously march directly into the gas chambers, boasting about their eagerness to inhale poison until the bitter end.

OK, so it's not a perfect analogy. Jews and other Nazi targets didn't go willingly.

So what kind of analogy *does* work? Masada? Jonestown?

It seems the mass hysteria we're witnessing today isn't unprecedented, but the scale of it seems to be. Especially since the usual path is for the deluded to attack others, not themselves. Of course, mask-deniers inevitably take neighbors and friends down with them and, as we saw on January 6, delusional people can also strike out against anyone.

I expect we'll soon be adding COVID comparisons to our bag of extreme analogies.

"These people are behaving like the self-deluded collaborators who refused to wear masks back when COVID wrought havoc across the globe…"

Freedom is essential for a humane society, no question, but "liberty" doesn't mean "anything goes."

The U.S. government orders us to pay income and property tax. Whether or not we agree, these are mandates we can't shrug off. We're told to obey speed limits, to not drink and drive. We're mandated by law or company policy to wear other bits of cloth in public—you know, like pants or shirts.

During wartime, the government drafts every healthy man to risk life and limb in battle. But wearing a mask for fifteen minutes in a store is an infringement of our rights?

"Can't fight fascists today. I'm binge-watching *The Walking Dead*."

During WWII, Americans in coastal cities were required (i.e., mandated) to use blackout curtains so enemy bombers couldn't see light coming from our windows. No patriots rallied at protests shouting, "I have a right to let Nazis target the whole city because I choose to give away our location!"

Unfortunately, even Holocaust and COVID analogies are insufficient to illustrate our mass inaction in response to the climate crisis. We're not talking about a few hundred people drinking Flavor-Aid or a few million refusing vaccines. We're talking about billions of people *allowing* our climate to become so inhospitable to thousands of species (crops, animals, pollinators) that although we might not go extinct ourselves, the survival of our civilization is another matter.

Sure, it's corporate owners and the politicians they buy who do the most serious climate damage, but if the rest of us *let* them get away with it, our behavior will soon be fodder for analogies that surpass either Holocaust or COVID comparisons.

Assuming history books or other forms of cultural communication still exist.

"It was like that time when, for *decades*, people just kept on pumping out greenhouse gases, even as they watched wildfires burn entire towns, and terrible floods disrupt major cities, and crop failures starve millions, and the collapse of the Gulf Stream devastate an entire continent, while doing nothing substantial to address any of it."

I used to feel offended by certain Holocaust comparisons. I still do, I suppose. But given the enormity of what we're facing now, those analogies may soon feel almost quaint. We'll need something that combines both the horror and cruelty of the Holocaust with the manic stupidity of COVID denial.

When a wall of flame is racing toward us at sixty miles an hour, we don't have time for incremental approaches. No "I'll trim the weeds this weekend" or "I'll buy a cistern when I get my holiday bonus check."

We can be disgusted by neo-Nazis. We can be baffled by the stupidity of mask-deniers. We can ridicule them if it makes us feel better.

But let's stop being stupid ourselves and stop voting for *anyone* who doesn't take the climate crisis seriously. Let's rally. Let's protest. Let's march. Let's petition. Let's boycott. Let's demand divestment. Let's donate to people and organizations who can lobby and pressure Congress *now*.

And, for God's sake, let's stop walking straight into the greenhouse gas chamber thinking maybe *we'll* get refreshing water, even as we smell the smokestacks belching out the ashes of our families.

Are We 'Catastrophizing' if We're Really in a Catastrophe?

We are warned against exaggerating, against hyperbole, against seeing events in the worst possible light. "Stop catastrophizing," we're told again and again. Things aren't that bad. In fact, things are better for more people now, we hear, than in any time throughout human history.

But are we catastrophizing if we're truly in a catastrophe?

Just how dire the threat of fascism is in the U.S. might be debatable, but that debate feels semantic. Perhaps the barrel hasn't gone over the edge of the falls just yet, but the fact that it's only 200 yards upstream doesn't quite prevent the situation from feeling serious.

With homelessness rising and rents increasing, with more people declaring bankruptcy because of medical debt and more young people afraid of earning degrees to avoid a lifetime of student loan debt, with the richest corporations gaining record profits while small businesses continue to flounder, perhaps it's an "exaggeration" to say that late-stage capitalism is a catastrophe.

Perhaps we look at our home and see a few missing shingles. Maybe we see peeling paint and a leaky gutter. A chip on the front steps. And we say, "What a disaster."

But is that really the same as seeing flames shooting out the lower windows, with our family beating at the windows upstairs, their escape blocked by iron bars?

As climate activists have repeatedly pointed out, we're acting as if the climate crisis is equivalent to peeling paint when instead it's a burning house.

We're told we're being melodramatic, that we're neurotic to see the climate crisis in such dire terms. We're paranoid. We're mentally unwell.

But isn't it crazier to insist that things are okay, that we can work on the fire destroying our home a little at a time, while the flames consume our curtains, our sofas, our children?

Is it crazy to pick up the spray bottle we use to chastise our cat and think we're doing something constructive to save our house?

Is it crazy to sit at our computer typing a letter to the editor or signing a petition while the flames shoot through the doorway into our office?

When do we justify catastrophizing?

More importantly, when—and how—do we convert the recognition of catastrophe into constructive action?

The metaphor, as useful as it is, can only go so far. We aren't all going to run out of the environment screaming. We can't just grab the baby, a handful of mementos, and meet other family members in the prearranged safe place.

There is no safe place. It's not our "house" that's burning. It's the entire neighborhood. We're the Marshall subdivision near Boulder. We're Abbotsford in British Columbia. We're Paradise in California.

And even this isn't a perfect metaphor. But let's not allow that to trap us into inaction.

If our house or our town was literally on fire, a school strike wouldn't *really* be our immediate course of action. Neither would a climate conference. Or a rally in front of City Hall. But all these things are important if insufficient.

Personal sacrifices aren't the answer, either. Even if everyone who believes the climate crisis is real never flies on an airplane again, are we all going to give up our cars? Almost none of my friends who understand the gravity of the situation are willing to do that.

I'd certainly encourage folks to promote public transit, but many of us started doing that decades ago, and there's been virtually no progress made in public transit or climate policy in the years since. Much of what we try may not work.

But if we're trying to escape a burning building and one pathway is blocked, we don't give up. We keep looking for another pathway.

We push for divestment from fossil fuels. We stop electing politicians who are not fully committed to meaningful action on climate. We stop making excuses for politicians who promise but fail to deliver, who "compromise" our future into mass extinction.

And if there's no one better to elect?

More of us need to consider running at least in local elections.

We can't rely on others to do the job for us. A heartbreaking video shot on a cell phone shows South Korean students on a sinking ferry discussing the instructions they've just heard over a loudspeaker to remain in place and wait for further direction.

"In movies," one of the students says, "the people who follow instructions end up dead and it's only the ones who disobey who survive."

Over three hundred students who followed instructions and waited for rescue died.

Our house is on fire. Our town is burning. Our ship is sinking. Whatever metaphor we choose, we can't accept, "Hang tight and wait for rescue."

There's no one right answer. The problem is so large it will require multiple approaches simultaneously.

But let's *not* catastrophize about our chances of winning an election or how our visit to speak with our elected officials will go. *That* kind of catastrophizing drains energy from the actions we need to take.

And let's not feel so insignificant that we excuse ourselves from the battle. To throw out yet another metaphor, it might well be *our* work, being added to that of millions of others who are already working, that becomes the straw to break the camel's back.

Or breaks a glacial dam, allowing the glacial lake behind it to wash away denial downstream.

Our efforts matter.

We're in the middle of a disaster of catastrophic proportions. Let's choose a course of action. And let's act. And act. And act.

Workers Quitting Crappy Jobs Should Also Quit Crappy Political Parties

I voted for Reagan in 1984.

By 1988, I'd registered as a Democrat and have voted for Democrats in every election since. I'm now canceling my membership in the Democratic Party.

I realize this means I can no longer vote in some primaries. But the decision to block open primaries is controlled by the major parties, as is the decision to block ranked-choice voting.

They also control the choice to keep the filibuster.

And the choice to maintain the Electoral College.

And the choice to allow gerrymandering.

And the choice to accept corporate donations.

I wish the best for those still trying to change the system from within. But when even our "heroes" on the left cave, time and time again, to corporate Democrats, I simply can't muster the energy to believe that "next time," they won't pull the football away at the last second once more.

If it's Democratic voters and not the Democratic Party machine destroying the chances of Nina Turner, India Walton, Charles Booker, Bernie Sanders, or others trying to make a real difference, this is still a group I no longer want to be part of.

So I'm out.

"But you can't do anything from the outside!"

That's probably true. But I clearly can't do anything significant from the inside, either.

President Biden had a chance (still does, and he absolutely will not use it) to cancel all student loan debt. If the DNC wants me back, they can see that he does so.

When Democrats control all three branches of government and still can't add vision and dental to Medicare, they're of no use to me. The DNC knows what to do if they want me back.

But I don't think they do want me back. I think they don't care about me at all. At best, they'll keep demonizing the "my way or the highway" voters, never accepting responsibility for their own position—"Let them eat cake crumbs!"

"Republicans are worse!" Democrats argue manipulatively.

I concede the point.

But if my options are to accept one broken leg or two broken legs, I'm choosing not to play this abusive game anymore.

I call my senators and representatives and council members, I send emails, I sign petitions. I mail postcards to voters in swing states. I donate to candidates who make promises and when they don't deliver, I explain why I won't donate to them again.

Since none of that seems to matter, the only thing left is to withdraw my membership. If "every vote counts," I can only hope that "every party membership" counts, too.

When winning on a no progress platform makes Democrats believe that making no progress is acceptable, when losing on a minimal progress platform makes them think they were too radical, when losing after capitulating on a high progress platform makes them think that zero progress is a more secure path to success, there is no way for voters to persuade party leaders we want more.

As Democratic leaders fumble in the dark trying to interpret voter behavior, every outcome justifies their decision to abandon even weak attempts to address our needs.

Of course, they really don't have to guess what their lower numbers mean. We've been telling them for years. They simply won't listen.

So what's the solution?

Party officials must demand that elected leaders pass meaningful legislation. We need universal healthcare, universal pre-K, equitable public school funding, tuition-free college and vocational training.

We need zero-fare public transit, with massive investment in public transportation and high-speed rail. We need significant and measurable anti-racist policies. We need to ban all fracking and new fossil fuel projects immediately and focus on healthier ways to power our cities.

"Be patient!" we're told, election after election after election. "Progress takes time!"

But science hasn't yet found a way to lengthen the human lifespan an additional three hundred years. I have no more patience because I have no more time.

With increasing economic inequity and an escalating climate crisis, even young voters don't have time to be patient any longer.

If Democrats can't get us the minimum we need to survive, culture war victories are only window dressing, "rights" that can be ripped away at any moment.

Because "compromise" for Democrats always means "we'll try harder next time," and because "next time" always means "never," I'm done. I've emailed the DNC, verified my name is no longer on their rolls, and demanded they remove me from their mailing lists as well. Any of their emails still coming to my inbox will be marked as spam.

Because that's what they are.

The Great Resignation needs to include leaving any political party that only pays lip service to our needs.

For all those Democrats upset with my decision, let me calmly reassure you—my membership was never going to lead to progress anyway.

Go Fund Yourself!

"Why do you rob banks?" someone once asked a notorious criminal.

"Because that's where the money is."

Any time progressives point out the need for Housing First to address our out-of-control homeless crisis, or the need for universal pre-K, or universal childcare, or universal healthcare, or fare-free public transit, or tuition-free college and vocational training, or a rapid transition away from fossil fuels, the complaint is always, "Where are we going to get the money?"

No one asks that when we give the military $768 billion. Or when we give subsidies to fossil fuel companies. No one questions the multitude of other corporate handouts we give away regularly.

Even more mystifying, no one asks how much it will cost if we *don't* create these programs.

But let's put all that aside and just answer the question. Where *are* we going to get the money?

We're going to get it from the only source that has it—corporations and wealthy individuals.

We can never raise the necessary money from sales tax. We can't raise it by only requiring income tax from the bottom 90% of the population. We can't raise it by increasing property taxes on middle income folks.

I earn $30,000 a year. My federal taxes are roughly $5000 and my property taxes a little over $3000. That amount won't even begin to help the three dozen families living in cars and campers in my neighborhood, much less address any other problems within a one-block radius.

We're *not* funding essential programs by squeezing the life out of poor, working class, or even middle class folks.

The wealthy, and the politicians they "donate" to, tell us we need to pull ourselves up by our bootstraps. In other words, "Go fund yourself!"

Do we "need" universal childcare? Do we "need" all public schools to receive equal funding? Do we "need" universal healthcare and tuition-free college and vocational training?

Only if we *don't* want to live in a rapidly failing society.

Sure, we can step over homeless people sleeping on the sidewalk. We can live with a system of mass incarceration imprisoning more citizens per capita than any other country on Earth. We can suffer under a healthcare system that places life expectancy in the U.S. below that in forty-five other nations.

But the fact that we *can* accept widespread poverty and misery doesn't alleviate any of that poverty and misery…or its consequences.

If raising taxes on the wealthy did nothing for me personally but only ensured that the thousands of unhoused individuals and families in my city had safe lodging, I'd be fine with that. If raising taxes on corporations didn't help me personally but did ensure that trash cans in public spaces were emptied regularly and that portable toilets and shower facilities were available to the unhoused, I could get behind that.

I don't need to benefit personally from the money raised from the wealthy and corporations to recognize the benefit to society. Because I'm part of society, and I *do* benefit. We all do.

It's great not having to sidestep human feces. It's wonderful to see toxic superfund sites in my city being cleaned. It's fantastic to see a vibrant public transit system helping transport folks to their jobs, to medical appointments, to visit friends *and* know that public transit is better than private vehicles in adapting to a worsening climate crisis.

We're not asking corporations and the wealthy to scrub our bathtubs. We're asking them to do what *we're* doing—pay their fair share.

If their personal share is larger, then their fair share is larger, too.

"Where will we get the money to fund essential programs?" you ask.

From the only source that has it.

Freedom isn't free. Equity isn't free. And a healthy, functioning society isn't free, either.

Yes, we can back the two major political parties and their corporate agenda, but that won't help us avert climate catastrophe or even the collapse of our nation. The tensions pushing us toward civil war are fed by widespread and increasing misery among millions of families of every political ideology.

Telling us to fund ourselves isn't a solution.

Americans have needs that must be met, and if our elected officials don't meet them, people will take their frustrations out on each other. Republicans blaming Democrats, or Democrats blaming Republicans—or defectors from their party—won't change that reality.

A few rich people at the top will probably survive even a cataclysmic civil war, but the rest of us had better understand quickly that, left, right, or center, our only real enemies are those who pit us against each other so they can keep all the resources for themselves.

People go to war for oil. They fight over water. Money to solve societal problems is a resource, too.

Who are the selfish here? People who want an education, a job, and to live above the poverty line? Or those who hoard more money than they could ever spend in a thousand lifetimes?

Even a minimally acceptable quality of life has a price tag.

Someone has to pay that price. And it can only be those who have the money to pay.

We don't want *all* their money. We only want everyone to pay their fair share.

We must tax corporations and the rich.

A Tale of Two Parties

It was the worst of times; it was the worst of times.

One of the leading political parties of the age fought actively against providing the people with healthcare and paid leave to spend time with their newborns. The other leading political party pretended to be for these things but almost never managed to pass any substantial legislation, even when they were in power.

One of the leading political parties advocated openly for the widespread dissemination of guns. The other party claimed to be for some modest degree of background checks, some tiny limit to accessing weapons able to kill large numbers of people quickly, but never managed to pass any substantial legislation, even when they were in power.

It was the worst of times; it was the worst of times.

One of the leading political parties blamed poor people for being poor. They created policies leading to an explosion of homelessness. They fought against raising the minimum wage so that workers had a fighting chance at finding even inadequate housing. The other leading political party claimed to care about the poor but endorsed almost all of the same destructive policies. They advanced "affordable housing" that no one making minimum wage would ever have a chance of renting, much less owning. They refused to make the changes necessary to improve conditions, even when they were in power.

One of the leading political parties was pro-police and pro-military, insisting on larger budgets year after year. They defended even the most blatant abuses of power, blaming unarmed civilians in the U.S. for sleeping in their own beds or driving with a broken taillight. They blamed civilian victims in other nations for looking too much like enemies. The other leading political party claimed to care a great deal about justice at home and abroad and yet continued to vote for these increasing budgets, continued failing to address any of the underlying problems, failed to hold anyone accountable or make any meaningful changes, even when they were in power.

It was the worst of times; it was the worst of times.

One of the leading political parties fought openly to privatize public education for children and limit access to higher education from the masses. The other party said they wanted to increase funding for primary education and make higher education "more affordable" but never managed to pass any substantial legislation. They promised student loan forgiveness but never quite got around to it, even when they were in power.

One of the leading political parties openly plotted to destroy democracy, gerrymandering to such an extent that they controlled most state legislatures even when most of their citizens voted for members of the other party. They openly curtailed mail-in voting, openly eliminated polling stations, openly led an insurrection on the nation's Capitol. The other party pretended to want democracy but refused to eliminate the filibuster, sabotaged primary winners on their side they didn't like, yet stood firm on vital issues again and again…until they gave in, even when they were in power.

It was the worst of times; it was exhausting *and* the worst of times.

One of the leading political parties denied the existence of a deadly virus, denied the efficacy of a life-saving vaccine, promoted unproven and sometimes dangerous therapies for something they still claimed didn't exist. They refused the simplest of efforts like masking to curb the spread of the disease. The other leading party pretended to believe in science but then refused to provide the vaccine to billions of people, allowing the virus to continue mutating into ever more dangerous forms. They refused to waive the patent for the various vaccines so that other nations could provide the vaccine for themselves. They refused to provide rapid at-home testing, even when they were in power, ensuring that friends and families of both parties would continue to infect one another

One of the leading political parties denied the climate crisis, even as the nation—and indeed the entire world—reeled from disaster after disaster. They contaminated groundwater, promoted pipelines that spilled, cut down forests the world needed as carbon sinks. The other leading party pretended to care deeply about the climate crisis but still promoted drilling and fracking, encouraged the burning of forests as a "net zero" solution, made vague promises for the distant future without ever taking action that could prevent the Earth from reaching a tipping point, even when they were in power.

It was the worst of times; it was exhausting, maddening, and the absolute worst of times.

Followers of one of the leading political parties decided that everyone not just like them was a mortal enemy who needed to be destroyed. Followers of the other leading political party certainly hated followers of the first but spent most of their time fighting each other rather than finding a solution to even one of their own party's problems.

Yet there was a growing number of people from all ideologies and walks of life who finally began realizing that a sustainable future could never exist under either of the two leading parties. Many of them weren't sure if the answer was Democratic Socialism or Marxism or some other form of socialism. Many demanded total loyalty to their new personal beliefs, risking authoritarianism instead of salvation when it was needed most.

It was the worst of times; it was time for a fundamental shift in American political and economic life.

Whatever course of action we choose, it cannot be a continuation of the status quo. Because the status quo doesn't exist. What exists is an escalating deterioration.

We've had years to reflect on what works and what doesn't. We no longer have decades to continue reflecting.

Let's be sure to make the best decisions we can without wasting any more time, while there still *is* time. One day, perhaps, someone will write an account of this age of turbulent change, and how eventually, despite the worst of human nature, we found the best in ourselves and worked together to create a better world.

Stop Moderate-Splaining!

Democrats are primed to lose in the mid-terms because Biden and the Squad have moved the party too far to the left. At least, that's what moderate pundits tell us day after day. If we want to save democracy, they insist, we *must* return to the sane, sound principle of governing from the middle.

As a white cisgender man, I'm frequently oblivious to mansplaining and whitesplaining, but when I hear ridiculous punditry about the importance of "moderation" from corporate media, I finally get it.

Stop moderate-splaining!

As reporters and analysts try to understand why Biden's popularity is so low, why the country hasn't learned its lesson from the disaster that was the previous administration, it's almost laughable to hear their reasoning.

Manchin and Sinema can't go along with Democrats anymore because the Dems have become too radical. If only the Democratic Party would get back in line, everything would be fine.

Folks like Cori Bush, AOC, and Nina Turner have other suggestions. "Forgive all student debt. Every penny."

And this is where framing becomes important. It's not that analysts are truly confused about Biden's low ratings or the impending defeat of Democrats in the mid-terms. The defeat could almost certainly be avoided simply by giving people what they need—universal healthcare, a higher minimum wage, tuition-free college and vocational training, and other human-centered programs.

Even given the limitations of working with Congress, there are policy changes Biden could make via executive order. There are policies Pelosi could back instead of pooh-poohing. It's not that we're only getting lip service. We aren't *even* getting lip service.

No one can snap their fingers and make the world perfect. But hiding behind "it's complicated" ignores the reality of what we could do now…if we *wanted* to.

The real question Democratic leaders are asking is, "How little can we do and still manage to stay in power?"

That's the debate. Is there a way to win back public trust without banning elected officials from stock trading?

Can forgiving a small percentage of student loans assure people we're on their side? Can we merely *say* something inspirational about racial justice and still keep most of the black vote?

There's no question what would win voters. There's no question what would help the country as a whole and the individuals in it.

Just as men often cut off women by calling them "hysterical," just as white people talk over "unpolished" people of color, moderates try to cut off human-centered policies by labeling them "radical" and "extremist."

We let Democrats get away with offering happy, peaceful quotes from MLK while ignoring his calls for socialism. We let mainstream media get away with depicting the Black Panthers as a terrorist organization.

The options then are calm, "polite" ideas or meaningful change. The "let's just be patient" side—moderate and mature—or the "people have needs *now*" side—crazy and dangerous.

We're told there's a "rational" perspective and a "fringe" perspective. The framing itself establishes the winner.

In recent years, thankfully, more of us are calling people out when they inaccurately frame the debate.

Stop mansplaining.

Stop whitesplaining.

And stop moderate-splaining!

Let's point it out when our friends and family do it, when our coworkers and neighbors do it, when reporters and politicians do it.

Concepts are easier to understand and communicate when we name them. They offer a framework upon which we can then attach examples that illustrate our position. Let's not worry about finding a perfect word, and let's not hide our meaning just to be clever.

We must defang the word "moderate" to stop fetishizing it.

Because the Democratic Party is corporate and capitalist, it's unlikely to ever address our needs, no matter what we say. Party leaders are fully aware they don't plan to help and so frame arguments as they do hoping to keep us from realizing it, too.

But if we call out the moderate-splaining when it happens, we can help move voters further to the left, where ultimately any hope of saving democracy and creating a society where we can all thrive remains.

Climate Inaction in Action

“9-1-1. What is your emergency?”

“A wildfire is heading straight for our house!”

“Are you in immediate danger?”

“Well…yes! The fire’s heading this way!”

“How far off are the flames? How long before they reach you?”

“I don’t know. We’ve never had a wildfire here before!”

“I can only help if you let me. Can you at least guesstimate?”

“For Pete’s sake!”

“Is that your final answer?”

“With the distance and topography, I’d say maybe two or three hours.”

“Excellent.”

“Excellent!?”

“You seem to have plenty of time to evacuate.”

"But there are only two ways out. One is already blocked by flames!"

"And the other?"

"I can't tell from here. The fire could get there before we do."

"But you're not sure?"

"Send us some help!"

"Please calm down. Getting hysterical is counterproductive."

"Oh my God."

"Yes, there is power in prayer."

"Can you *please* send some firefighters?"

"Firefighters and equipment cost a lot of money."

"I pay my taxes!"

"But the CEOs in town don't."

"Just send what you can, okay?"

"Those fire engines burn a lot of fossil fuel, you know."

"I…I…"

"Oh, stop making such a fuss. You haven't even *tried* evacuating yet."

"I don't want to lose my home and everything in it!"

"Good grief. Losing your house isn't the end of the world."

"Help us!"

"Okay, okay. Listen, do you have a sprinkler system in your yard?"

"Yes…"

"Excellent. Turn it on."

"We're in a drought. The timer is controlled by the city council. We get half an hour of water twice a week."

"Hmm. I passed the golf course on my way to work this morning. It looked green enough."

"Can you activate our sprinklers from your location?"

"I'm afraid not. But how about this? I can make a call to the city council—an urgent call, tell them it's a priority—and ask them to raise your water allowance."

"What!?"

"Sure. We'll get you *four* days of sprinkler usage a week and increase your allotment to an hour each time."

"Are you out of your friggin' mind!? The fire will be here in two hours!"

"Don't exaggerate. You already said it could take up to three hours."

"We need help *now*!"

"I'm calling the city council on another line as we speak. I'll get them to turn on your sprinklers before the end of the workday."

"Today's Saturday."

"I'll leave a message *and* send an email."

"I…I…"

"No need to thank me. This is what we're trained for."

"Please…"

"I'll put the subject line in all caps."

"Can. You. Please. Send. Some. Firefighters!?"

"Don't you worry. I'll call the After Hours line, too, while I stay on this line with you. You won't be alone. And your sprinklers will be on again before you know it. Plus, I hear the City is about to sign a new contract for better water service any day now. Better filters and everything."

"But…"

"Oh, someone's picking up. I just need a moment to explain the situation to them."

"Tell them to send helicopters!"

"Ah, it's voice mail."

"Tell them…tell them…"

"You might want to pull your window shades down while you wait. That'll deflect some of the heat. Do you have any white paint around the house?"

"Oh my God! The flames are getting so close! They'll be here in thirty minutes!"

"You *said* you had *hours*."

"For the love of God…"

"Please hold."

The World's Most Extraordinary Income Inequality

Recently, my husband and I began watching a Netflix show called "The World's Most Extraordinary Homes." My husband's a former builder and frequently tunes in to various programs on HGTV. We also enjoy a British series called "Grand Designs."

While some of the other shows reveal an enormous amount of entitlement—"I could *never* live in a house with only five bathrooms!"—other aspects make them tolerable. But this "Extraordinary Homes" series is a slap in the face to humanity.

Imagine the luxury of a walled-off home on the Israeli coast, complete with heavily watered landscaping in a country that's 60% desert, with a built-in swimming pool, only miles from Gaza. These particular homeowners may be fine people, but the immorality of an economic and political system that allows such extreme differences in living conditions for its citizens is impossible to ignore.

As viewers, we're supposed to celebrate the wonders and beauty of what we're seeing.

I'm watching in horror.

It's not that I don't appreciate beautiful architecture. I own books showing "Five Hundred Buildings of Paris" and "Five Hundred Buildings of London." When I lived in Italy, I loved going to the Coliseum in Rome, even knowing it was a place of death and misery. I marveled at the beautiful cathedral in Florence. I'm aware that almost every incredible building ever constructed came at the cost of exploiting the humans who built them and lived in their shadows.

But it's one thing to appreciate architectural marvels from history and another to actively cheer and encourage exploitation and abuse in real time. Even the former is problematic, like saying, "Well, that elephant has already been killed, so I might as well enjoy its ivory."

I've watched several episodes now of what I call "The World's Most Extraordinary Income Inequality." Weekend homes in India with floor space five times my primary (only) residence in privileged America. The owners can't even be there most days, working miles away in Mumbai, where over seven million people live in slums (55% of the city's population). One of the homes featured in the episode showcased an elevated swimming pool, high above the ground to keep the snakes and rats out.

Could there be a more accurate depiction of the dystopia created by capitalism?

All that said, I can't help but recognize my own privilege. I do live in a house (the bank still owns most of it, but in relative terms, it's "mine"). I have a television, and cable. I stream Netflix. I have a job. I have electricity.

I may be poor compared to the folks living in the luxurious homes on this television show, but even I'm a pampered aristocrat to those seven million Mumbai residents living in abject poverty.

Everything's relative.

But that's the problem with this and similar shows. We're watching the top few percent of the world's elite, while those handful at the top keep pulling farther and farther away from the rest of us.

It's like watching a departing spaceship carrying the world's richest man.

We can enjoy the trip vicariously, exclaiming in delight at every well-designed, beautiful feature of the extraordinary properties. Everyone needs a little escapism, right?

But at the very least, let's use what we see to strengthen our resolve to ensure that housing is officially considered a human right. Let's work for Universal Basic Income. Let's campaign for tuition-free college and vocational training so that more folks living in poverty have at least a fighting chance to rise above it. Let's finally establish Medicare for All or some other form of universal healthcare so that tens of thousands of families in the U.S. don't lose their homes to medical debt every year.

Those battles are exhausting and it's okay to treat ourselves a bit so we'll have the strength and courage to continue.

Perhaps tonight, I'll watch an episode of "Snowpiercer" or "Squid Game" while eating some genetically modified, monoculture popcorn.

I'm a Diabetic Afraid of Needles, and I'm Triple-Vaxxed

I hate needles. No one in their right mind *likes* them. I've even passed out—twice—after getting jabbed.

When I was 10, I had to get a four-needle TB test. A few minutes later, I stood beside my mom and said, "I don't feel so good." The world started turning green, and the next thing I knew, I was on the floor.

Eight years later, I had to get a flu shot before sending in my papers to volunteer as a full-time LDS missionary. I was sitting on the edge of the exam table and thought, "How interesting. That's the same color green I saw when…"

The next thing I knew, the doctor was trying to revive me.

In Rome, my zone leader volunteered the missionaries to donate blood for one of the local church members. I was grateful the phlebotomist allowed us to lie down. I didn't pass out.

Shortly after I returned to the States, my mother developed leukemia, and I donated platelets to reduce her bleeding. Apheresis involves taking blood out of one arm, spinning it in a centrifuge to separate out the desired component, and putting the rest back in the other arm. It can take a couple of hours each time.

I loved my mom, I hated needles, and I did what I had to do.

Several years later, I came out as gay and left the Mormon Church. AIDS was raging and blood banks refused to let gay men donate, even if they didn't have HIV. I was happy to have an excuse to avoid another needle.

I remained HIV negative for the next twelve years. Then I made a single mistake and…

I joined a medical trial as soon as I tested positive, even though it required blood draws every six weeks. The phlebotomist drew 15 vials each time. After 24 blood draws over the next three years, you'd think I would finally get used to needles.

But I didn't. I still hated them.

After that, I continued having blood drawn every four months for the next several years. It never got better.

Of course, HIV meds led to side effects which led to other prescriptions which led to additional side effects. I thoroughly understand wanting to avoid medications of any sort whenever possible. Nothing comes without a price.

I began getting flu and pneumonia vaccines regularly, and I kept up with my tetanus shots. My great-aunt died of tetanus, and I assure you, you don't want tetanus.

When I was finally eligible for a shingles vaccination, I rushed to get both doses. A good friend of mine in his forties had shingles. I assure you, you don't want shingles, either.

As I grew older, I eventually developed diabetes. I only needed pills at first and decided that once I needed to start injecting, I'd simply kill myself instead. Facing needles every day the rest of my life sounded like a life not worth living.

Then I needed daily injections.

It turned out that insulin needles are tiny and don't hurt much.

I gave up bread, a pain far greater than any needle I've ever felt.

But I eventually needed two daily injections.

And you know what? IT SUCKS!

It's not so much the needle but the constant bruising. And if you aren't careful, you end up with scarring and permanent lumps. My thighs and abdomen are covered with them.

Every morning, I swab a fresh spot of skin and meditate while waiting for the alcohol to dry. I position the needle and then…and then…and then…I inject. I see people who just lift their shirt, stab, and they're done in three seconds. Not me. It takes me a couple of minutes every day because I still hate needles.

As a gay man who lost several friends to AIDS, I understand not trusting the medical establishment. I read *Good Intentions: How Big Business and the Medical Establishment Are Corrupting the Fight Against AIDS* back in 1990.

When a healthcare system's primary purpose is to make money, when treating or healing the sick is secondary or tertiary, there's plenty of reason to distrust doctors and drug companies.

That said, waiting until the healthcare system is perfect means never seeking medical care at all, and I'm not willing to return to the cave dwelling era.

I got a COVID vaccine the moment I was eligible. Then I got my second dose. And then I got my booster. Three shots over the course of a year. About a day and a half in diabetic years.

Yes, we should get capitalism out of healthcare. We need Medicare for All or some other form of universal healthcare. But in the meantime, let's stop allowing phobias (of needles, of doctors, or of anything else) to keep us from protecting ourselves and those we love.

Parents Who Believe in Sexual Purity Should Still Vaccinate Their Kids Against HPV

With all the talk about COVID vaccinations, we forget that there are other useful vaccinations out there, too.

"My children don't need to be vaccinated against HPV," I've heard some of my Mormon friends and family say. "They'll still be virgins when they get married. They'll never have to worry about an STD."

Apart from the vindictive "people get what they deserve" mentality of such a belief, the truth is that our kids don't need to be sex addicts to become infected with one of 40 sexually transmitted human papillomaviruses that can lead to cervical, vaginal, anal, vulvar, oral, throat, and penile cancer.

First, let's establish some norms for this discussion: science is real, hormones are real, lapses in judgment are real.

If our son or daughter has a single momentary lapse, has sex just one time before marriage and then quickly and sincerely repents and never has sex again until marriage, do we not believe in forgiveness?

What if our son or daughter is still a virgin on their wedding day but they marry someone who isn't? Maybe their spouse only had one lapse or perhaps they had several. But they've repented and they're committed to sexual monogamy. Maybe our son or daughter doesn't even know about their spouse's past.

Let's add a few other basic norms for this discussion: some people lie convincingly, some people don't consider omitting important information dishonest, some people are too ashamed to reveal parts of their past.

Are we still okay with our child getting cancer as a punishment for something they didn't even do?

Another unpleasant reality is that 1 in 5 women and 1 in 16 men will be sexually assaulted while in college. Rapes occur on religious campuses as well. Even at BYU.

I've heard some parents say that *their* child would fight to the death to avoid being raped, that no one is really raped without at least partially consenting.

What I've *never* heard is the parent of a missing child say they hope their child has been murdered in addition to being raped.

Kids get overpowered and raped. Adults do, too. So do the elderly.

If our child has been traumatized by such a horrific event, do we really want to penalize them even further with the lifelong knowledge they might develop cancer later as a result? That they could infect their future husband or wife?

Aside from these scenarios, we should also recognize that our children may simply choose another path in life than we want for them. They may choose to have multiple sex partners. Do we truly want to see them die for their views on sexuality?

There's a difference between "tough love" and "tough vindictiveness." Perhaps we aren't participating directly in "honor killings," but are we guilty of honor manslaughter? Honor child neglect?

What if all our children and their spouses are virgins when they marry and none of them are ever sexually assaulted? Are we *then* finally able to justify our refusal to vaccinate them?

Some marriages end in divorce, and we find ourselves dealing with the sexual history of the new partner, if there is to be one.

What if the marriage ended because our child's spouse had an affair?

What if our children have wonderful, successful marriages in every way possible, but then their spouse dies in an accident or from cancer or some other illness?

We're back to dealing with yet another partner's sexual history again.

Not every infected person shows symptoms. Not every infected person develops cancer. Some just develop warts. Is *that* something we're okay with inflicting on our loved ones, just because we can't accept they'll ever have sex, either consensually *or* non-consensually?

Some people are opposed to all vaccines. There's no convincing those folks. But most of us are okay with vaccinating our kids against measles, mumps, rubella, tetanus, and many other harmful viruses.

Can we so easily allow our fear of sexual sin to put the lives of our children at risk, when that risk can be greatly reduced with a simple vaccination?

If a physician must take an oath to "do no harm," I hope that we as parents can make the same commitment to those sacred souls entrusted to our care.

Is There *Anything* I Can Say to Get You to Donate?

If you're like me, you get a hundred or more fundraising emails every day from corporate and "centrist" Democratic candidates. They offer dire predictions about the end of civilization as we know it if we don't send our money their way NOW!

To be honest, the situation *is* dire, but more often than not, these folks aren't the solution.

Two incumbents I supported in the last election cycle reneged on their promises, so they've lost my support until *after* they deliver. Once you're in a position of power, no matter how minor, you must do more than *say* the right thing.

Others running for the first time may or may not follow through on their promises, but they at least need to make those promises if they want my money.

When I receive these manipulative fundraising emails blaming me personally for the end of the world, I have a short response saved in a Word document that I cut and paste into my reply.

Let me explain why I bother.

Years ago, I went out on a date that ended poorly. When the guy called later to set up another date, I declined. Years passed before we ran into each other again, and he wanted to know why I had dumped him.

"You don't wear deodorant."

He'd thought I hadn't found him attractive, that the reason might have been X or Y or Z. He'd racked his brains trying to figure out what he'd done wrong. The answer had seemed obvious to me. Surely, he knew that most people wore deodorant and that stinking could at least theoretically be a turnoff for some people.

But he needed to hear it.

It's hard for me to believe most candidates don't read polls and understand that the "center" is far, far to the left of where most centrist candidates are. Do I really want to vote for anyone so clueless?

But even if they do know, it won't hurt for them to hear it again. And it's useful to tell them why *we* aren't donating. They're not mind readers. They might think they're not far *enough* to the right. So when we can, let's give them our reasons. Even if only one low-level staffer or volunteer reads our reply, that's an important message reaching someone who needs to hear it.

I recommend coming up with your own reply, as there are obviously many valid points to make besides the ones I've mentioned. But here's a template to get you started:

You asked if there was "anything" you could say to get me to donate to your campaign.

Yes! Yes, there is!

You could come out in support of Medicare for All, tuition-free college and vocational training, a ban on all fracking and new fossil fuel projects.

You could come out in support of fare-free public transit (and more public transit).

You could come out in support of subsidized childcare.

Yes! There are plenty of things you could say to get me to donate to your campaign!

I'm still waiting for you to say even one of them.

Please do so while there's still time.

I have limited funds and can only donate to candidates who meet the bare minimum requirements. I don't have enough to give to every "lesser evil" out there.

Please let me know when I can donate to your campaign!

Thank you!

Few of us have the stamina to reply to every single fundraising email from dozens of lackluster candidates. We're all busy and stressed, without enough time to compose these replies over and over, day after day. But with a pre-written text, sending even a couple each day is worth the few seconds it takes.

There are plenty of essential yet time-intensive and energy-consuming political actions to take if we want to save democracy (and the planet) but dedicating five minutes a day to a Cut and Paste Reply session is something even the busiest among us can squeeze into our schedule.

Do You Smell Smoke?

A gubernatorial candidate's slogan is "Jesus. Guns. Babies." She proudly announces she wants a theocracy in America. Elected officials call their political enemies "demons" and "reptilian lizard people." They claim that those who disagree with them are cannibals, aliens, robots.

Over and over, those on the right—the mainstream right, not the fringe—call everyone else "evil, evil, evil." Anyone on their own side who disagrees, perhaps a former presidential nominee like Mitt Romney, maybe a former vice president like Mike Pence, are demonized for displaying any hesitancy. They're "traitors."

Meanwhile, we watch as our friends, neighbors, and coworkers take prom photos in the park, bicker over a tennis court reservation, follow the latest celebrity gossip.

We joke about the stupidity of those plotting our destruction.

As if nothing was wrong.

In a college psychology course years ago, I learned of an experiment in which a subject was observed in a room by himself as smoke was gradually introduced through a vent. If the subject was alone, he jumped up and reported the smoke almost immediately. If, however, other folks were in the room—actors who were part of the experiment and told not to react—the subject would look around in confusion. Seeing that no one else was concerned, he'd wait until the room was thick with smoke before he finally took action.

Even in another version where none of the three subjects was in on the experiment, they each still waited far longer than if left to make a judgment on their own.

If the problem was serious, *someone* would do something about it, right?

When I came out as gay, a member of my extended family promised to hide me "if they ever come for the gays." Now she supports the people targeting me.

For years, center-left journalists pointed out the dog whistles in political statements from those on the right. When rightwing officials say "urban," they mean "Black." When they say "globalist," they mean "Jew." A hundred different dog whistles.

Now, though, candidates, pundits, elected officials, and justices have given up the dog whistles. They're stating their goals out loud. "We've won on abortion and we're coming after birth control." "We must overturn gay marriage." "We don't want everyone to vote."

They're making it a felony to be homeless.

They label everyone opposed to their complete takeover of government "enemies of the state" and "Satan worshipers."

It's not only easier to kill traitors than neighbors—it's a moral and legal necessity.

Words matter. Like yelling "Fire!" in a crowded theater.

We smell smoke. We *see* the smoke. But the folks around us go on about their day as if nothing is wrong. So we doubt ourselves. Maybe that mist will dissipate on its own. We don't want to look like idiots by making a fuss.

Or be accused of channeling Orson Welles and causing a *War of the Worlds* panic.

We're afraid even to talk about it with our partners, among our friends. We might induce a contagious yawn and all start to cough.

We don't want to cough when we're hiding.

Besides, behaving as if this is real only gives the right more ammunition. Emboldens them to take action. We can't let them smell our fear.

As a recent meme pointed out, "The road to fascism is paved with people telling you to stop overreacting."

We don't need to guess what those on the right "might" do next. They're *telling* us. We should believe them.

We smell smoke when we see the world's most proudly capitalist country failing at providing basic necessities like healthcare. And education. And baby formula.

We smell smoke when we see worsening droughts, floods, storms, and heat domes. But presidents and prime ministers don't seem concerned. Maybe we're imagining that smoke.

Or...perhaps we should accept the evidence right in front of us and *do* something.

Find a better system than capitalism.

Stop creating new fossil fuel projects.

Believe that those on the right are coming for us.

And act accordingly.

Before the air is so filled with smoke we can no longer find a way out.

The Cultiest Two Years of My Life

Ex-Mormons debate whether or not The Church of Jesus Christ of Latter-day Saints is a cult or simply a religion with dedicated followers. For me, there's little doubt that any organization—religious or political—which allows no room for diversity of thought is a cult.

Mormons, already forced into narrow molds, are virtually prisoners during their two-year "voluntary" missions. LDS missionaries are assigned "companions" who they must stay with every hour of the day and night. You might get a few minutes in the bathroom by yourself, but you're forbidden from locking the door, and the head missionary in each apartment can walk in on you unannounced to make sure you're not masturbating. Some mission leaders even require male missionaries to sing hymns while they're in the shower to reduce the chance they'll feel tempted to touch themselves.

In some missions, presidents confiscate the passports of the missionaries serving under them "for safekeeping."

As missionaries, we weren't allowed to watch TV, see movies, read newspapers, read any book not published by the LDS Church. We weren't allowed to call home. We weren't even allowed to study our new language more than half an hour a day because we needed to devote our time to more spiritual matters. We *were* allowed to listen to music, though—cassette tapes of the Mormon Tabernacle Choir.

I did my two years in Italy, much of that in Rome. Our leaders taught us that the Catholic church was the Whore of Babylon, that we were special and valiant and that's why we'd been called to serve on Satan's doorstep. A false, mystical sense of superiority is almost always part of cult behavior. Everyone wants to believe they're special.

Every single day of my mission, our "district" (the four or six elders living in each apartment) had a morning devotional. We prayed, sang hymns, and shared our plans and goals for the day. This wasn't just a warm morning chat. The following morning, we were taken to account.

"You said you were going to teach a lesson. Why didn't you? Were you goofing off? Why didn't you have the Spirit with you to get inside someone's apartment? Were you sinning?"

We were given a weekly goal that was virtually impossible to achieve. In fact, in the two years I was a missionary, only two companionships ever reached their weekly goal. Once each.

We all knew the goals were ridiculous but if anyone suggested as much out loud, we were immediately shot down. "You're letting Satan whisper in your ear." "You're a Doubting Thomas." "Only those who have real faith make it to the Celestial Kingdom."

Visiting leaders from other parts of Europe spoke to us a couple of times a year. One of them told us during a zone conference (each zone comprising about a third of the missionaries in the mission) that "If you had faith even as a grain of mustard seed, you could each baptize five hundred people a month."

Even rudimentary math showed that 120 missionaries x 500 was 60,000 converts a month, just in our mission alone, and at the time, the LDS Church had four missions across Italy. That would be 240,000 converts in the country every month. By the end of my two-year mission, we'd have converted 5,760,000 people.

Even today, forty years later, there are barely 20,000 Mormons in all of Italy.

No one believed we could accomplish something of that magnitude, and not only because we taught that all people possessed free will. I could see the looks we gave each other, the missionaries who started to whisper to their companions but stopped themselves. The numbers were preposterous, but we didn't want to be the one to bring the entire mission down with our lack of faith.

That inevitable lack of faith was an important tool. Because we didn't—couldn't—achieve the success demanded of us, we "knew" we were terrible sinners and therefore had to do whatever else possible to atone for our failure. Belief in our inadequacy was necessary to keep us under control.

At the end of each week, we had to fill our "stat sheet" with our goals and actual numbers. Then we had to write a letter to the mission president. We handed the letters to our district leaders, who read them before passing them on to the zone leaders, who read them before passing them on to the Assistants to the President, who read them.

The mission president himself didn't read them unless someone had inadvertently included a red flag of some sort that necessitated an urgent call to repentance. We quickly learned to avoid any problematic wording.

During the quarterly zone conferences, after we listened to all the pep talks, every single missionary in attendance was required to bear their testimony that they knew the Church was true. The meeting would not end until everyone had spoken. The silence between testimonies could drag on for five or ten minutes. Weary missionaries who did not want to bear their testimonies finally stood and swore their belief just to be done with the ordeal.

But we still weren't done. We each then had to participate in a personal interview with the mission president behind closed doors.

Some missionaries loved zone conference. "A day off from work!" But most of us would have knocked on a thousand doors to avoid the torture.

I'd signed up to be a missionary because I was a true believer, shocked once I was "in the field" to discover that many of the others didn't believe at all. They came because their parents refused to pay their college tuition unless they put in their two years. Perhaps their father promised them a car. Or their girlfriend refused to marry them. Some of the sister missionaries came looking for a husband. Some of the elders just wanted to escape their suffocating families back home.

Imagine the family environment that could make mission life feel free in comparison.

Whatever our motivation, once we were "called," there was no turning back. To leave early meant being labeled a loser. We risked being disowned, losing all our friends and family. One of my early companions did ask the mission president if he could return to America. The president refused, so my companion paid a prostitute for sex and forced the president to send him back. Another elder sneaked out of the apartment and headed to the airport, but the other missionaries called the mission home, who sent out the Assistants to head him off before he had a chance to board the plane.

They were "saving" us from making a terrible mistake, doing us a favor by keeping us there against our wishes.

Not every day was terrible, of course, though parts of every day were. I enjoyed many wonderful experiences during my two years. But I also fantasized about running off and living as an Italian. I stood at the railing of a ferry from Sardinia for two hours contemplating jumping into the sea. One of my companions almost threw himself in front of a commuter train.

RMs (Returned Missionaries who have completed our missions honorably) enjoy a special status in our congregations. Missions are a two-year hazing that grant us membership among the privileged "worthy" for the rest of our lives.

As long as we never question anything even after we return to civilian life.

Of course, we're assured we *can* question, but if we don't come up with the right answer, we're obviously listening to the wrong spirit and need to repent. And to keep us from having the time to question much in the first place, we're encouraged to marry and start having kids as soon as possible. We're called to new volunteer positions in our congregations that we're often unqualified for, providing more fuel for our feelings of inadequacy.

While missionaries, we're told that our mission will prepare us for the rest of our life. "Conditioning" might be a better word. Many of us suffer Stockholm syndrome for decades after. Missionaries I was sure would go "inactive" within months of their return to America are still stalwart members forty years later.

"My mission was the best two years of my life." The assertion is so common it's cliché among Mormons.

And yet, as awful as the experience was for me, it was also incredible. I learned a new language that I still speak four decades later. I learned a new culture.

I learned that there was a world beyond my hometown, beyond America. I became a global citizen during my mission and have tried to remain one ever since. I've studied French, Spanish, Russian, Hebrew, and American Sign Language. I've read dozens of books in Italian. I listen to Italian and Spanish pop music. I subscribe to MHz and watch programs from Italy, France, Switzerland, Germany, Portugal, Norway, Sweden, Denmark, and Turkey in their original languages.

I married another ex-Mormon who served his mission in Rome. We speak Italian every day.

Leaving the cult wasn't easy. My husband's bishop ordered him to find a young woman and have sex to "straighten" himself out. His LDS counselor ordered him to undergo electroshock torture.

My husband refused to comply with either suggestion.

My own LDS counselor ordered me to read the book *The Unhappy Gays*. He ordered me to speak with an ex-gay minister.

I did both and was so horrified by the blatant lies and warped thinking that instead of retreating, I came out fully. When my stake president called me one evening and said, "Your church court is in half an hour. Did you want to attend?" I immediately headed over. I had no doubt about the outcome but was curious to see how it functioned.

At the conclusion of my Court of Love, when I was told I was being excommunicated, the stake president informed me, "You must remove your garments now."

I had long since stopped wearing Mormon underwear—they're not especially sexy when you pick someone up at a bar—but was struck yet again by the extreme control the Church had over us. They chose our underwear and even told us when we could and couldn't wear them.

The cultiest two years of my life offered me the chance to question authority for the first time. So while those years may not have been the "best," they were perhaps among the most important.

I'm sixty years old now and can attribute many of the best decisions I've made to the New and Improved "me" that developed during that trial by fire. But I can't quite recommend the experience to anyone else. Better to volunteer in our own communities teaching English to immigrants or delivering meals to shut-ins or building houses with Habitat for Humanity. Better to do a year abroad in college, volunteer with the Peace Corps, or just travel and stay in hostels in a dozen different countries.

I'd encourage old and young alike, believers and non-believers, to contribute as advocates and activists to improve the lives of others here and abroad by finding ways to address the climate crisis, passing universal healthcare, demanding tuition-free college and vocational training. Cults are strongest when there is need, so our best defense against their damage is to alleviate psychological and physical need. And dedication to any movement that improves lives can offer the benefits of missionary work with far less of its psychological damage.

Of course, I've seen similar types of groupthink in some of these movements, have watched friends defend their moderate or left or far left political parties with the zeal of fanatics. Some defend their charity of choice from any criticism, no matter how well deserved. Cult behavior exists because humans are susceptible to creating cults and being victimized by them.

In the end, the best we can do is be aware, teach ourselves and our children how to think critically, and understand that some people *like* having an authority figure make decisions for them. We'll never live in a world free of cults, so we'd better learn how to function and progress even in their midst.

Make Christians Christlike Again

After I was excommunicated from the Mormon Church, most of my friends cut me off. "It hurts too much to know our eternal friendship won't endure past this life," several told me.

The shunning was painful, but now as I watch conservative Christians heckling the President about his dead son, mocking children who choose to wear face masks, investigating the parents of trans kids for child abuse, and chanting in favor of a dictator invading a sovereign nation, all I can think is, "Please, shun me! Stay as far away as you can!"

Not all Christians, not even all conservative Christians, behave in these horrific ways, and certainly there are plenty of non-Christians who behave poorly as well. Still, the vitriol spewed from conservative American Christians may well prove as damaging as radioactive fallout from a sabotaged reactor.

They pose holding Bibles in one hand and guns in the other, with goofy grins plastered on their faces. Warm, fuzzy intimidation. Sweet, wholesome death threats.

The giddy gleefulness with which some of these conservative Christians taunt their victims feels anything but Christlike. Making fun of school shooting survivors, coughing in the faces of immunocompromised neighbors, and calling 9-1-1 on children selling lemonade don't feel quite as righteous as a widow offering her last coin to charity or Jesus defending a woman accused of adultery.

For Mormons, there's an added perversion. We were taught that in the Pre-Existence, we were presented with two plans. One of God's sons said he'd come down to Earth and *make* people be good. Another son said he'd come down and atone for their inevitable sins.

Forcing people to do God's will, we were told, was wrong.

All the more bizarre then when Mormons join other conservative Christians in celebrating climate disaster and the portent of nuclear war because these catastrophes might usher in the Second Coming, as if God somehow needs *us* to force *his* hand.

This conservative Christian collapse into cruel, delusional behavior has been evolving for decades. Given the history of the Crusades, the Inquisition, slave trading, lynching, and even mere shunning, it's clear, of course, that some degree of Christlike love has long been deficient.

Lately, though, there's been an escalation in its deterioration. Conservative Christians spouting vicious insults have become the Holy Shit of *Mean Girls*. Mocking disabled reporters, gloating when unarmed protesters are killed, shrugging when our leaders boast of sexual assault.

We smile as we hurt others. We laugh as we crush. We betray with a kiss.

What would Jesus do?

The New Testament unequivocally tells us that the Savior would devote most of his energy worrying about the genitalia and hormones of athletes. He'd worry about the gender of children's toys.

He wouldn't waste time on war refugees. Or those displaced by climate change.

He wouldn't worry about finding homes for the unhoused. Or providing healthcare for the sick.

In his Sermon on the Mount, Jesus stated, "Blessed are those who lie for the Lord, for they shall be made writers of alternate scripture."

"Blessed are those who torture in the name of love, for they shall inherit self-satisfaction."

"Blessed are the bullies, for they shall be angels in the world to come."

"And blessed are the heartlessly sadistic, for theirs is the kingdom of heaven."

To be honest, I find it difficult to understand why anyone would *want* to follow a God they believed was asking them to behave so repulsively.

Thank God I was shunned.

Please, in the name of all that is good, keep shunning me!

At least until you find a way to help make Christians Christlike again. If you need any help, there's always that other son of God whose plan *wasn't* chosen.

You know him as the Devil.

And you seem to know him quite well.

Let's Celebrate Higher Gas Prices

People are being murdered in Ukraine to fulfill the pathological needs of a dictator. We watch as children lie dead beside the road, as apartment buildings are bombed, as old women stumble over rubble trying to escape the shelling with their little dogs.

"How terrible!" we say.

"How awful!"

"Someone should *do* something!"

And then our gas prices start to rise as we cut Russia off from one of its major funding sources.

We *care*, we insist, but not enough to put up with *that*.

It's easy to criticize those complaining as shallow and selfish, and some of them undoubtedly are, but most of us are drowning in blood and oil as it is because our own government is led largely by egocentric oligarchs, too.

Financial advisers often ask, "Are you putting enough away to retire comfortably?"

One of my employers confided his personal worries to me once during his lunch break. “Do you think I can retire on a million dollars?”

I put a whopping $25 aside every two weeks. I’m not going to say how much I have in savings, but it’s considerably less than a million dollars.

And I retire in two years, the moment I turn sixty-two.

Why don’t I and millions of others like me not put more into retirement accounts? Why don’t we plan better? Do we not understand the ramifications?

It’s not unlike the questions climate scientists ask us every day.

We’re concerned, obviously, with the bills due *now*. Who has time or energy to worry about a future we can barely imagine?

No one wants to pay more for gas. We don’t want to pay more for “greener” food choices. And we don’t want to support corporations we know are abusing employees and raping the environment, but we can’t afford to shop elsewhere.

Like millions of other Americans, not only do I *not* contribute significantly to my savings, but I’m instead often forced to withdraw funds to cover unexpected bills.

Still, my days as an employee *will* come to an end, whether I have any savings left or not.

We *will* kill bees and other pollinators if we keep using bee-killing pesticides.

We *will* increase global temperatures by 3 degrees Celsius if we keep using fossil fuels.

We *will* as a result face worldwide "retirement" without enough environmental savings to get us through the lean years ahead.

Many retirement experts advise clients like me against taking Social Security too soon. It's better to wait until we're sixty-five or sixty-seven.

So why don't I plan to wait?

Because the recent IPCC reports show that irreversible climate damage might occur before I reach a more appropriate age.

There will soon be no option for any of us to delay facing the consequences of our lack in planning.

On my own, I can't stop climate change by giving up beef or wearing my clothes until they disintegrate. Those kinds of individual efforts amount to a drop of oil in a tanker carrying 8,000,000 gallons. $25 twice a month trying to reach a million dollars in two years.

Any meaningful change must take place on institutional and governmental levels. Religious organizations can commit to installing solar panels on all their roofs. Cities and counties can require building owners to paint any roofs not fitted with solar panels white.

The federal government can ban all new fossil fuel projects. It can invest in solar, wind, wave, algal, thermal, and other types of energy production and storage as well as carbon capture.

It can certainly ban fossil fuels from countries attacking and killing innocent civilians.

One thing we as individuals *can* do, though, is stop bitching about the price of gasoline.

Gas prices will soon be the least of our worries. As any Ukrainian can tell you, any Syrian, any Chechen, any Yemeni, any Lebanese, our normal lives and concerns can change in an instant.

So let's welcome higher gas prices as an opportunity to demand that our leaders—local, state, federal, athletic, network, religious, and food conglomerate—make the institutional changes necessary for all of us to reach a healthy retirement age and have a fighting chance to enjoy it.

Can We At Least Get a Proxy Apology?

Leaders of The Church of Jesus Christ of Latter-day Saints have consistently refused to apologize for past teachings deeming Black members of the Church inferior. Current leaders say they can't apologize on behalf of long-dead prophets. They want to look forward, not back.

But one can't move forward after past mistakes without making amends, whether the harm done was intentional or not. And that can't be done without an apology.

If we can do temple work for the dead, baptize the dead by proxy, perform marriages for the dead by proxy, we can certainly apologize for the dead by proxy.

Previous Church teachings told us that Blacks had been "fence sitters" in the Pre-Existence. They were less valiant and cursed with a dark skin to warn the rest of us to keep our distance. Black males, no matter how worthy during their mortal existence, could not hold the priesthood.

This wasn't merely a "priesthood ban," however. Without the priesthood, Blacks could not take out their temple endowments, could not partake of temple marriage, and as a result could not fill the prerequisites for entering the Celestial Kingdom, the highest level in heaven.

That's apart from Church members being allowed to own slaves, even donate a slave as tithing in one case. And that's also separate from Church teachings on Native Americans, advocating for *their* enslavement as well, and other problematic policies on race.

When Mormons go to the temple to do work for the dead, we're aware that we aren't forcing folks in the Spirit World to "accept" the work. They continue to exercise free will, can still say, "Yes! Thank you! I accept the baptism!" or "No, but thanks anyway."

So why is it so hard to apologize on behalf of former Church leaders who taught and practiced such harmful theology? We aren't forcing them to accept the apology made on their behalf. We're simply allowing them a chance to make some tiny effort at repairing significant harm.

These apologies are *already* being offered by proxy. Individual Church members—lots of them—are apologizing for the sins of the past. They do it through a petition on change.org. They do it in person to Black members in their congregations. They do it by funding films about LDS members in Africa.

It's important for us as individuals to apologize. Like it or not, we accepted harmful teachings. We believed our leaders without questioning.

We *should* have questioned long ago, long before the "Race and the Priesthood" essay, before we were given permission to think differently. "I was just following orders" has been the justification for most atrocities throughout history. We don't get a pass just because we "believed" the orders.

We don't like to think we're capable of hurting others. We didn't *mean* to hurt anyone. So we often try to shift the responsibility onto someone else. That's a natural first reaction.

It's a problem, though, when that's the end of self-reflection and repairing the harm we've done.

But even as more and more of us come to understand systemic and institutional racism, as we come to understand unconscious bias and struggle to make changes in our personal lives, in our workplaces, and in our relationships, we still understand that individual efforts alone are inadequate, just as individual efforts to reduce greenhouse gases cannot succeed in mitigating global warming without direct action by corporations, institutions, and governments.

It's not that individual efforts don't matter. They're essential. They're simply *not enough.*

Black members of the LDS Church need an official apology. All of us need to hear—officially—that current Church leaders apologize for discriminating against Blacks *and* for teaching white members to discriminate along with them.

Years ago in my Single Adults group, a friend explained why he wouldn't date a certain young woman. "She's active in the Church now," he said, "but she *used* to be inactive."

"So you don't believe in Christ's atonement?" I asked.

"Oh, she can be forgiven for what she did," he said, "but I don't think people ever really change."

Genuine repentance is more than saying we're sorry. It requires change as well. But a change in behavior without the apology, without making amends, isn't repentance, either.

When LDS leaders refuse to apologize, they aren't "looking forward." They're sending a clear message, fully understood by their Mormon audience, that the people harmed simply aren't *worth* apologizing to.

It's still a continuation of racist theology, and that continuation has consequences.

LDS Church leaders must stop deflecting and apologize. If they can't bring themselves to apologize for their own behavior, they can at least offer an apology by proxy.

Coats When It's Cold, Masks When There's Virus

COVID infections are skyrocketing again. Thankfully, there's only a modest rise in hospitalizations and deaths, but those "modest" numbers would have seemed horrific two years ago. Many "lighter" cases still have people sick and miserable, missing work or infecting coworkers, isolating from family or infecting loved ones.

But since mask mandates have been lifted almost everywhere, most of these people will *not* wear one. "I don't have to!" they insist.

No, they don't. But there's no law preventing them from *choosing* to wear one.

When I was a Mormon missionary in Rome, the male missionaries had to wear suit coats whenever we left our apartments, even if it was blazing hot outside, until May 15th each year, when the mission president deemed it was now warm enough for us to take them off.

He made that decision *for* us because we, as young men, were too stupid to know if we were hot or cold. The sister missionaries had no such rule. They could wear sweaters, or not, as they saw fit.

Once, I broke a raw egg in the pocket of my suit jacket—don't ask—and removed the jacket at church. My local missionary leader ordered me to put the coat back on. It was "inappropriate" for me to remove my suit jacket at church.

Today, while on my commute to work, while I'm interacting with coworkers and customers, I think back on those ridiculous rules and make the obvious connection. When it's cold, coats are useful. When there's an uptick in viral infections, masks and distancing are helpful.

Last week, one of my coworkers, still sniffling, told me she was just getting over her second case of COVID this year. She was conscientious, wearing her mask at work…under her nose. Several other coworkers have come down with COVID more than once, even when masking was mandatory. Not a single one of them wore their mask over their nose at work back then and almost none of them wear a mask at all now.

Masks don't work, they'll tell me. People are tired of the pandemic, they say.

I ride public transit to and from work, three hours a day, with folks who don't mask, with folks who do, with folks coughing non-stop, with folks sneezing, with folks eating and drinking and talking loudly on their phones, with mentally ill folks screaming at the top of their lungs.

So far, despite my risk as a frontline worker, my risk riding public transit, my risk interacting with unmasked coworkers, I've avoided even one bout of COVID. I tend to believe masking, social distancing, and vaccination have helped.

Coworkers who have done one or two but not three of these have almost all come down with COVID.

Perhaps I will, too. Perhaps it's inevitable.

But I don't have to get COVID *today*.

Each infection with COVID carries a 20% chance of developing long COVID. That's a percentage worth avoiding.

Many of my friends have grown tired of the pandemic, tired of masking and distancing. Over a dozen of them have become infected in the past couple of months.

Every year when winter comes, I put on a jacket when it's cool. I put on a coat when it's cold. When it's warm, I take my jacket off.

When I'm walking outdoors, I take my mask off. When I'm alone at work, I can remove it if I want to. When I'm near other people, I put my mask on.

No one has to give me orders. I am perfectly capable of making this decision on my own.

It's impossible to avoid all illness but *reducing* the number of illnesses we suffer is easily achievable.

If you're one of those people whose job duties prevent you from wearing a mask, that's one thing. But if you're just "uncomfortable," that's another. Sure, you can decide that the misery of COVID infection is less for you than the misery of wearing a mask. That the moral responsibility of stopping the spread of a still-mutating virus rests with someone else.

But that's certainly not my decision.

My mission president used to decide when I wore my coat.

My employer used to decide when I wore my mask.

I make those decisions for myself now. You can, too.

I Scream, You Scream, We All Scream for Pronouns

"I don't use pronouns."

When I heard a coworker make this odd announcement during an employer-assigned study group, I was at first confused. The English teacher in me wanted to stop the lesson and ask everyone to diagram my coworker's sentence.

The employee who introduced himself next said almost the same thing. "I don't have pronouns."

The following employee agreed. "I don't use any special pronouns, either."

I finally understood the problem. People who asked others to use pronouns that didn't coincide with the gender they presented were demanding special rights. Trans or non-binary folks were so different that these coworkers couldn't even acknowledge they ever used pronouns themselves under any circumstances.

Pronouns like "I," for instance.

Wives clearly never referred to their husbands as "he." Husbands never referred to their wives as "she." Parents never referred to their children as "they."

It wasn't the ignorance my coworkers displayed about basic parts of speech that surprised me. I did teach college English for ten years, after all. And we're all ignorant about something until we learn about it.

It was the disdain that surprised me. Because the mandatory study group was about equity and social justice.

We've all kept misgivings about new workplace policies to ourselves as a matter of self-preservation. We might complain bitterly to friends later or, if a supervisor directly asks for feedback during the meeting, a brave few might provide it.

But most of us are savvy enough not to go into a meeting about home mortgages, for instance, and say, "I don't believe in special loans just so people can be housed."

In our meeting on social justice, my coworkers and I began with a land acknowledgement. Our study group was being conducted on stolen land. That day we were to discuss colorism. At a previous meeting, we'd discussed misogynoir. Every employee in the organization had been assigned short articles and videos so we'd be better able to understand the basics of that week's topic when we met in groups of ten to fifteen participants. I felt happy to be working for an organization that was at least making an effort.

I'd been called the N-word on public transit a few days earlier, though my skin was barely a shade darker than alabaster. When the bigot finally paid enough attention to realize his error, he began calling me a "fucking [f-slur]" instead.

Nothing more than a crazy person on the bus?

Perhaps.

But more and more, people across the country feel emboldened to "tell it like it is." And the truths they reveal are a profound animosity toward LGBTQ folks, toward ethnic and religious minorities, toward women, toward people of color, and toward workers.

That's a lot of people.

Hundreds of anti-LGBTQ bills, attempts to deny women access to healthcare, and voter suppression laws have been proposed—or passed—just in the last few months. Many more are on the way.

Those in power, including everyday folks belonging to the dominant culture, use a divide and conquer strategy as one of their many weapons to keep everyone else "in their place."

They use the strategy because it's effective.

While one group is fighting off attacks on bodily autonomy and reproductive choice, another is fighting off attacks on a trans woman's access to public restrooms. Yet another is fighting for the right to unionize. Some folks are fighting for the right not to be killed during traffic stops.

Others are fighting to stop the rape, trafficking, and murder of indigenous women.

There's more than enough to keep any one of these groups fully occupied.

But the only way to resist these attacks is to work together. The three white, cisgender men at my workplace who dislike LGBTQ folks so much they can't even be bothered to learn what a pronoun is need LGBTQ folks to back labor laws. People of color need white folks with disabilities as allies. Women—or people with uteruses—need gay Latinos on their side.

If we allow our unconscious biases to be weaponized by our shared oppressors, we all suffer. This isn't a zero-sum game where we can sacrifice trans folks to get gay rights, where we sacrifice black men to get better working conditions for Asian women.

You don't like everyone in the various targeted groups?

You don't need to.

When I was a missionary, I didn't like every other missionary I met.

When I was in nursing school, I didn't like every single one of my classmates.

In forty years, I've never worked a job where I liked all of my coworkers.

I don't even like everyone in my own family.

This isn't about liking everyone or approving of every choice other people make.

It's about joining forces for our common welfare. If we want rights for ourselves, the only way to guarantee them is to make sure everyone else has rights, too.

That's not a philosophy or ideal. It's reality.

So let *us* commit to work together, no matter what *you* think of *me* or *I* think of *you.*

Because solidarity is the only way to survive this increasing onslaught of attacks on our lives.

This Isn't the New Normal. These Are the Good Old Days

If we dare turn on the news anymore, we see reports of record heat, flash floods, flash droughts. We see 34 million people displaced when a third of their country is inundated by record monsoons. We see reservoirs running dry, fire tornadoes, entire towns wiped off the map by wildfires.

There are as many climate disasters these days as there are mass shootings, and they take an even bigger toll.

"Record" becomes as meaningless a term these days when speaking of weather as "unprecedented" became years ago when talking about politics.

Some newscasters suggest this is the new normal. But it isn't. *These are the good old days.*

We're tired of hearing about climate change, tired of worrying, tired of unsuccessfully urging elected officials to do anything about it.

But being tired of something doesn't alter reality. I'm tired of injecting myself with insulin twice a day. But if I stop doing it, my A1C will shoot up to 10 or 11. The fact that I'm tired of needles and bruises and lumps doesn't change reality.

I'm tired of going to work at a thankless job. But if I stop working, the interest doesn't stop accruing on my loans. The late fees on unpaid bills won't magically stop piling up.

We're tired of lots of things but being tired doesn't change reality.

Action does.

"It'll cost too much!"

Does complying with building codes cost more than not complying? I suppose it depends on the final tab after we factor in having to rebuild the structure once it collapses, once we factor in the settlements to the families of those who were killed or injured in the collapse.

The cost is there, one way or another.

In any event, **price tags don't change reality. Climate disaster doesn't go away just because addressing it is expensive.**

King Midas was granted his deepest wish, for everything he touched to turn to gold. Unfortunately, when his food turned to gold along with everything else, he could no longer eat and starved to death.

In recent weeks, we've heard complaints when activists glue themselves to roads, glue their hands to the frames of paintings in museums, or glue themselves together in a chain around the Speaker's chair inside the House of Commons.

"It's not nice!" "It's disruptive!" "It's just theater!"

Well-behaved activists rarely make history.

Of course, making history isn't the goal. We're trying to ensure there will *be* history.

When I hear complaints such as these, coming from "the left" as much as the right, my response is always the same. "If you have a better idea, no one's stopping you."

Nothing anyone's tried yet has forced a decrease in greenhouse gases. While critics wait for the perfect, polite solution, others are desperately trying anything they can think of. Some of those attempts will be offensive. Some even harmful.

"But please," I tell complainers, "if you know what works, do let us in on the secret!"

The task ahead feels overwhelming. It's easier to pretend it's not as urgent as we know it really is. Otherwise, we end up battling depression along with everything else. And that's not useful, we tell ourselves, so it's *good* to put it all out of our mind.

Let's imagine, though, we're at home asleep with our family when suddenly, we hear armed men breaking in. It's a home invasion.

We have a gun, but it's secured and unloaded so our youngest children don't accidentally shoot themselves. There's no time now to load.

What do we do?

Are the odds so daunting that we just shrug and give up? Do we hand over our spouse to be murdered? And then our oldest daughter? And then our oldest son? And then the rest of the children, including our newborn? Do we then hand over the dog to be butchered, too?

We don't even know if these armed men are trying to rob us or if they're targeting us for our race or political views. We could "cooperate" with these powerful men and hope for the best. Sometimes, that turns out okay. Maybe we'll "only" be raped or beaten and not killed.

Is that a chance we're willing to take?

Or do we find *some way* to fight back? Do we grab a lamp, a baseball bat? Do we call 9-1-1 and barricade ourselves in our children's bedrooms, ready to fight to the death to protect them? Do we lower our kids out the window even if we're on the second or third floor, to give them a fighting chance with moderate injuries rather than injuries much worse if we do nothing?

Don't we try *something* to save ourselves and our loved ones, even if the odds seem insurmountable?

Perhaps we've followed the escalating crime in our neighborhood and have already built a panic room. Maybe we think we can ride out the home invasion without incurring any personal risks. We'll just keep quiet until the bad guys leave.

But what if the bad guys decide to burn our house down, whether to destroy evidence or simply out of spite, while we're trapped inside with our family?

Can we passively leave our fate in the hands of the worst people imaginable?

Perhaps we don't fight to curb global warming like our lives are on the line because deep down we don't really believe it's serious. Maybe we're closet climate change deniers.

Or perhaps we're just at a loss over how to do something "meaningful."

During WWII, we had Victory Gardens. We all agreed to put blackout curtains on our windows. We rationed.

In war, and sometimes even in peacetime, we institute the draft. We're forced to risk our lives for our country. Even if we claim conscientious objector status, we're required to perform some other kind of necessary, risky work to help the war effort. We don't just get to opt out and go about our lives as we choose while others sacrifice and die, merely because we have some distorted view of personal freedom trumping every other consideration.

Most of us are already convinced "something must be done." But we simply don't know what *we* can do personally.

We read articles and watch videos because we keep hoping that finally, someone will have "the answer."

But no one has the answer. **And everyone does.**

So what is it?

Do *anything!*

Do the right thing!

Do the wrong thing!

Brainstorm. Try ten wrong things. Fifteen. Thirty.

Doing nothing can't ever solve the problem, so let's do whatever we can think up, no matter how minor, no matter how silly others think our actions. Do it even if others think we're being counterproductive.

Don't let critics stop us.

If a home intruder comes at us with a knife, do we question our instincts? There may well be a dozen better ways to defend ourselves, but we can only use what we have available, and we have no choice but to do it *immediately*.

There's a time for research and planning, a time for rehearsal. And there's a time for action.

Let's try to make a difference in the climate battle using what *we* have at hand, which includes *our personality* and *our individual circumstances*. Let's try and fail if we must, try and succeed if we can.

Taking action on climate is bigger than embarrassment, bigger than guilt, bigger than shame.

No matter what anyone says, let's decide on something *we* can do, big or small, and let's *do it.*

Yes, I'm Offended and I Want to Sin

When members of The Church of Jesus Christ of Latter-day Saints leave, their former friends shake their heads sadly and gossip among one another. "She left because she was offended." "He left because he wants to sin." Many ex-Mormons become infuriated by these accusations, but I want to say for the record, "I'm offended, and I want to sin."

I'm offended that Latter-day Saint leaders refuse to apologize for the Church's history of oppression against black members (and non-members). That they refuse to apologize for past oppressive doctrines and policies against Native Americans, to acknowledge theology that demeans women. I'm offended they won't apologize for ordering the physical torture of LGBTQ students at their Church-run Brigham Young University.

Or that they refuse to discipline the member in good standing who helped design the US military torture program. In fact, they made the guy a bishop.

To paraphrase Celine Dion, "The list could go on and on."

But feeling offended isn't the only reason I left. I also want to sin!

I want to watch R-rated movies and TV shows with sex and language warnings. *Schindler's List. The Accused. Maurice. Wind River. The Handmaid's Tale. The Lives of Others.*

I want to read inappropriate books. Even if they contain four-letter words. Or awkward history. Or challenging questions.

My other sins?

I support the Equal Rights Amendment. I support marriage equality.

Even if advocating for fairness and justice *were* sins, I support the right of people to commit them.

Just as we have the right to be baptized or refuse baptism, the right to be married in the temple or instead at City Hall, to attend church or go fishing, I believe we have free agency in secular matters as well. We can accept medical treatment or refuse it, donate a kidney or not, donate blood or bone marrow or plasma or not, no matter the moral implications.

I support the right of people to acknowledge their gender and make decisions about their own bodies, even when it pertains to their genitals. I may not "approve" of someone's tattoos or piercings, but what they do with their own body is really none of my business. Just because *they* got a Prince Albert doesn't mean I have to.

Too many members of The Church of Jesus Christ of Latter-day Saints want to turn their personal decisions about their own lives into laws forcing everyone else to make the same decisions for theirs.

You know, like Satan's plan to force everyone on Earth to be "good."

A plan Mormons *say* God rejected.

Leaders of the LDS Church claim they don't want to be involved in politics but do feel obligated to speak on "moral" issues. Yet what qualifies?

They refuse to back universal healthcare. How can healthcare *not* be a moral issue, though, when they consider marijuana one?

I believe that Black Lives Matter, and I *don't* believe a righteous response to that sentiment is a murderous rage against the person who expressed it.

I believe housing is a human right, whether or not a person pays their tithing or stops smoking.

I don't accept that capitalism, a system that postdates the Bible and the events in the Book of Mormon by centuries, is ordained of God.

I believe that "not taking a stand" on fossil fuels and greenhouse gases is no better than Pilate "washing his hands" during the trial of Jesus Christ.

LDS leaders refuse to insist lawmakers ban assault weapons used to kill children at school, families at movie theaters, friends at music concerts.

But is enabling murderers with thoughts and prayers moral? To paraphrase Jim Lovell, "Salt Lake, we have a problem."

I'm confused that more people who claim to believe strongly in morality don't find it moral to right wrongs and make the world a better place now rather than wait for a messiah to clean up our mess at some vague, undetermined future date.

Leaving social justice up to God in the afterlife when we could do something about it ourselves in this life is a sin.

Despite my decadence, obvious in so many ways, *this* isn't a sin I want to commit.

And I'm offended that so many others in my faith tradition do.

Be a Jerk for Jesus

It's not just the Oath Keepers and Proud Boys and Patriot Front anymore. Countless new social clubs and religious organizations are sprouting up across the country to follow their lead. Liars for the Lord. Creeps for Christianity. Be a Jerk for Jesus.

Obviously, fanatics to any cause, religious or not, can be bad for society, but presently in the U.S., it is fanatical Christians posing the biggest threat.

One way to tell? They feel simultaneously offended and proud to hear anyone say so.

For Christians, there are two great commandments: "Thou shalt love the Lord thy God with all thy heart, and with all thy soul, and with all thy mind. This is the first and great commandment. And the second is like unto it, Thou shalt love thy neighbour as thyself. On these two commandments hang all the law and the prophets." (Matthew 22:36-40, KJV)

That second commandment is important enough to repeat: "Therefore all things whatsoever ye would that men should do to you, do ye even so to them: for this is the law and the prophets." (Matthew 7:12, KJV)

While many Christians claim to love God with all their heart, they seem to have misinterpreted "love" as "tough love." And it seems they consider "tough" to be synonymous with "cruel." Stranger still, this tough love isn't directed at God but at their neighbors, instantly weakening the misguided Christian's ability to adequately fulfill the second commandment.

Over the past few decades, the GOP and Christianity have become conflated, to the detriment of both. Christian political leaders try to deny school lunches to LGBTQ students. Others force women to carry dead fetuses in their wombs for weeks, force ten-year-olds to bear the offspring of their rapists. Still others accuse grieving parents whose children had body parts blown off by assault rifles of being crisis actors.

Cruelty is the point because the King James Version of the Bible has been replaced with a new and improved Republican translation. "Put the screws to your neighbor as you would put the screws to yourself."

Only they don't follow even their own revisionist doctrine.

Christian scriptures say, "Let your light so shine before men, that they may see your good works, and glorify your Father which is in heaven." (Matthew 5:16, KJV)

Does anyone honestly believe the targets of all this cruelty feel the least bit encouraged to glorify God?

"Hey! Did you see the way they ripped that family apart at the border? I'm on Team Jesus now! He sounds *great*!"

Almost every conservative policy reads the same way. Written as scripture, they become:

Sabotage your neighbor as you would have your neighbor sabotage you.

Despise the least of these thy brethren as you would have the least of these thy brethren despise you.

Deny your neighbor equal rights as you would have your neighbor deny you.

It's difficult for many Christians to understand they are victims of affinity fraud because that fraud *depends* on people trusting their manipulators *because* they are fellow Christians. But substituting even a few specific examples into the Biblical commandment makes it clear that the most important part—love—has been erased.

Stick it to your neighbor as you would have your neighbor stick it to you.

Be smug and self-righteous with your neighbor as you would want your neighbor to be smug and self-righteous with you.

Gloat over your neighbor's misfortune as you would want your neighbor to gloat over yours.

Applaud those who shoot your neighbor as you would have your neighbor applaud those who shoot you.

The list could go on almost indefinitely, since so many who call themselves Christian find endless new ways to make the lives of others miserable. Is it "mean" of us to point out the truth? Are we being "nasty" when the evidence is undeniable?

We'd happily adopt a live-and-let-live attitude if so-called Christians would do the same. But you're committed to crushing us as evidence of your Christian love.

Onward, Christian Bullies

The Church of Jesus Christ of Self-Centered Saints

Assholes for the Love of God

When right-wing leaders and pundits are called out for suggesting Christians shoot gays or liberals or unhoused people, they claim they're just joking.

Because God thinks jokes about murder are funny. Anthropomorphic thigh slappers. If we understand their underlying motivation is worship.

It might be worth investing a bit more effort into ensuring a separation of church and hate.

Or have I misread the Golden Rule? Is it instead to kill your neighbor before your neighbor kills you? Is *that* the gospel of Jesus Christ? The "good news"?

A Mass for Meanies

Bloodlust for the Lord

Jackasses for Jesus

I'm sorry for Christians who have been taken in by this affinity fraud. And I'm sorry for their victims. I'm sorry that we're *all* going to suffer because so many have been swindled into believing that the best way to prove their love of God is to hate their fellow man.

Let's sing the hymn together. We all know the words. "Jesus hates you, this I know, for the Bible tells me so."

As a former missionary, I have to say this type of outreach isn't effective.

But it's not really about outreach, is it? It's about proving to God who belongs in heaven. And what better way to do that than by making the lives of others a living hell?

As Christian writer C.S. Lewis once said, "Of all tyrannies, a tyranny sincerely exercised for the good of its victims may be the most oppressive. It would be better to live under robber barons than under omnipotent moral busybodies. The robber baron's cruelty may sometimes sleep, his cupidity may at some point be satiated; but those who torment us for our own good will torment us without end for they do so with the approval of their own conscience."

Members of almost every religion find themselves cherry-picking religious teachings to fit their personalities, and the bulk of American Christians are no exception. As we send our vitriolic pleas for the destruction of our fellow man heavenward, we ignore the most obvious passage from the New Testament:

"Many will say to me in that day, Lord, Lord, have we not prophesied in thy name? and in thy name have cast out devils? and in thy name done many wonderful works?

"And then will I profess unto them, I never knew you: depart from me, ye that work iniquity." (Matthew 7:22-23, KJV)

Lest we feel tempted to repent of our cruelty, though, and master kindness and empathy instead, let us remember a passage from the Republican version of the Bible and thus save ourselves from the dangers of charity and *agape*: "Let your hate so shine before men, that they may see your repulsive works, and be disgusted by any concept of God you offer as justification." (Matthew 5:16, RT)

On this hang all the laws of the damned.

Football Has Fans, Religion Exists, and Climate Change Is Real, Too

When I came out to a straight Mormon friend years ago, he reacted as positively as his cultural background would allow. "I don't understand it," he said, "but then, I don't understand why some people don't like basketball, either. I just accept that it's true."

My friend's reaction is a healthy way of approaching reality most of us could incorporate into our own lives.

I'm a former Mormon who is now atheist. Religion pretty much bores me, at least the way it's practiced much of the time. Yet ignoring religion because it doesn't personally interest me would be a mistake, since religious leaders perverting their influence negatively impact LGBTQ folks like myself, limit women's rights, make the lives of workers more difficult. They also shape cultural attitudes toward climate.

We can't ignore reality if we want to enact meaningful climate policies.

At the risk of offending sports fans, I'm not the least bit interested in soccer or football or baseball or hockey. Not even basketball like my Mormon buddy.

But I know that billions of people worldwide follow sports religiously. Whether or not *I* care about it, whether or not I understand why other people do, the fact remains that sports fandom is real. Universities devote huge portions of their budget to stadiums and training at the expense of academics. Governments orchestrate slave labor to build arenas. People spend thousands on game tickets, spend their yearly allotted vacation to attend playoffs. Fans even riot and kill over the outcome of these "games."

Sociologists devote their careers to mapping out the causes and effects of these phenomena. Lawmakers step in to mitigate the corrupting influence of gambling. Pastors and rabbis write sermons using sports analogies to persuade their congregants to practice spiritual principles.

Meanwhile, I grumble and groan when I'm forced to board light rail at the end of a tough workday and squeeze in beside hundreds of fans heading to the stadium. What could possibly possess people to waste so much time and energy?

Ignoring the reality of sports culture would be foolish. Yet my attitude toward sports is almost identical to that of millions of people worldwide who can't bring themselves to care about climate disaster. Those of us who do care are mystified by their disinterest, the same way my straight Mormon friend can never understand why I don't follow the Utah Jazz.

We need to individualize approaches to reach our friends and family to show them it's normal not to care about every single thing we do but *also* that their lack of personal interest doesn't alter reality. If it's not a moral failing to feel disinterest in basketball or numismatics or opera—or politics, for that matter—we must accept the reality that our friends and family who aren't interested in reducing greenhouse gases can still be caring, humane people.

Sometimes, because the issue is so important to us, that's a difficult concept. But we can't make progress without accepting this reality as well.

Granted, another reality is that some people are hemorrhoidal assholes who are completely unreachable. I hope we've already learned to distance ourselves from the trolls in our circle. But not everyone is a sphincter who isn't committed right this very minute to stabilizing our climate.

After all, *we* don't devote our lives to every single vital cause, do we? How many of us risk our lives and jobs fighting for racial equity? Or better representation for the disabled in media? Or tuition-free college and vocational training for every American who wants it?

There are too many important causes for everyone to feel the same on every issue. Sometimes, our friends and family have been deliberately deceived, too easily perhaps, but even that doesn't make us morally superior.

Everyone has believed something wrong, something damaging, at some point. We progress, we learn, we grow, and just because we're ahead on this one point doesn't mean our friends and family may not be ahead on others. If we believe in our hearts these folks are morally "less than" because they don't instinctively appreciate the severity of the problem, our scorn will come out in every interaction.

We must accept the reality that self-righteousness, even when we're right, damages the climate because it impedes persuasion.

Just as I need to plan my commute around sports traffic, we can help people unconcerned about climate understand they still need to make logistical concessions to its reality. Those concessions almost certainly include a ban on all new fossil fuel projects, perhaps rationing fossil fuels to encourage citizens to adapt to changing infrastructure, even diverting part of the military budget toward subsidizing renewable energy, since climate breakdown is an issue of national security.

People who are disinterested in climate issues don't need to *like* these adaptations. They don't even have to understand them. They simply need to accept reality.

So how do we reach Grandma? If she's a dairy farmer, let's try an analogy about milk production. If she's an accountant, perhaps a ledger sheet would work better. Our other friends and family might respond to analogies for gardening, yoga, *Game of Thrones*, or pottery.

Maybe they're not basketball fans but can't get enough tennis.

Let's find an analogy that meets our loved ones where they are. Because climate change is as real as homosexuality, whether we like it or not.

A Gastric Bypass for Global Warming

At twenty-five, I weighed 190 pounds. Horrified, I fasted forty days over four months while walking two hours a day and lost fifty pounds, which I kept off for another fifteen years. A success story by almost any measure.

This is where we as a civilization were decades ago as scientists who understood greenhouse gases and the corporate leaders who suppressed their research. The planet's "weight," or temperature, might have been managed at that point and kept under control. Even then, it would have taken a great deal of work, but it was possible.

After I turned forty, the number on my bathroom scale slowly began rising. While I preferred weighing 140, seeing 142 wasn't really a big deal, so I accepted it. I wasn't a kid anymore. Gaining a couple of pounds was natural.

As politicians, as corporate leaders, as voters, we began hearing that we should manage global temperature, but it didn't feel *that* hot, so we decided to worry about it later.

Before long, I weighed 145 pounds. That was still a healthier weight than most of my friends. I still looked good, could still pick up a cute guy when I wanted. Dad bods were "in." Life was great.

A couple of months later, I realized I weighed 147 pounds. But that was only two measly pounds above a perfectly acceptable 145. I'd lost my buffer but was still doing okay. I was sure no one else even noticed.

Denial is a normal human reaction.

As politicians, corporate leaders, and voters, we began noticing a few exceptionally strong storms, some troubling droughts, began recognizing that aquifers were shrinking, but if a crop failed in this state, we could always buy replacement yields from that state. It was annoying, but there was no real need to *worry*.

By the time I reached 180 pounds, course correction was already too daunting to attempt. Sure, I hadn't regained all the weight back, but losing forty pounds a second time was going to require an inordinate amount of dedication and effort, and I had a life to live. I was flying to New York and San Francisco and Paris and Rome. Losing weight would have to wait.

Then my husband got cancer, and all my energy went into taking care of him while working my regular job. Naturally, the weight continued to creep up.

We don't make great decisions when we're stressed.

After my husband died, a hurricane struck and I had to start my life over thousands of miles away. Finding an apartment, getting furniture, starting a new job, and trying to make friends consumed every bit of excess energy. I had no reserves for a weight loss regimen.

Internationally, we've had to deal with wars and invasions and rebellions. We've had to deal with recessions and monopolies and real estate bubbles. We've had earthquakes and tsunamis and pandemics and Reality TV.

And insurrections.

I developed diabetes and tried to cut down on carbs, but that meant increasing fats. The pounds kept piling on. My doctor warned me about heart attacks and strokes. I changed jobs, was laid off, found another job, quit, was unemployed, found yet another job, struggled to pay bills, and slowly got back on my feet.

When I reached 244 pounds, more than a hundred pounds over the weight I'd been when I stopped being careful, I realized I was powerless to make any meaningful change on my own. I needed help. An extreme intervention.

Globally, we're losing entire cities to wildfires, seeing towns wiped off the map in flash floods and mudslides, watching entire states, regions, and countries become deserts. We lose forests to pine beetles, coral reefs to rising acidity, suffer from the spread of mosquito-borne disease.

If we don't do something, the planet is going to suffer a heat stroke. Society will suffocate like a climate migrant in the back of a tractor-trailer.

After purchasing some compression socks and a larger pair of pants, I consulted with my physician and was soon enrolled in a bariatric program, planning for a gastric bypass.

That's major surgery, with serious, lifelong consequences, a risk of internal bleeding, a risk of additional surgery, even a risk of death. But I'd waited so long to address the problem that now only drastic action offered any chance at all of success.

Even "success" would never mean returning to 140 pounds. I'll be lucky to reach 180 after two or three years. With my new stomach the size of a hard-boiled egg, I'll never live a normal life, never eat a normal meal, never have a birthday when I can relax and eat so much as a thin slice of cheesecake followed by a single scoop of ice cream.

Never. Not even once. No matter the occasion. *It won't physically be possible.*

Humans can adapt when we must.

As politicians, as corporate leaders, as activists and advocates, as voters, as human beings, we have some serious decisions to make. Do we accept our planet's temperature obesity and the elevated risk of its disability and death without a fight?

Or do we fight?

The choice isn't only between a lower quality of life or death. There's also a third possibility—a lower quality of life *and* death.

In a best-case scenario, we're talking mitigation, survival. We've waited too long to fully recover. Thriving is no longer on the table. But that doesn't mean we don't still have options.

A gastric bypass for the Earth, combined with a healthy diet and appropriate medication, involves an immediate ban on all fracking and all new fossil fuel projects. It involves promoting public transportation over private vehicles, developing more efficient ways to harness and store wind, solar, wave, thermal, and other energy sources. It probably involves even more controversial measures, like a two-child limit or mass relocation away from doomed cities and regions.

It almost certainly means accepting that capitalism exacerbates rather than alleviates our problems.

Bypass surgery isn't *fun*. No one pretends it is. It won't make us "happy."

It's *necessary*.

Or…we can see just how obese it's possible to become. Some people, after all, have surprisingly good blood pressure even when they weigh 600 pounds.

We can visualize such a future, put an obese filter instead of a cat filter on all our video conference calls.

Instead of looking at the world through rose-colored glasses, we can see a future—a *present*—where every individual weighs as much as an entire family.

If that sounds like a horror movie, it's nothing compared to what awaits us if we don't act.

The Earth's climate needs a gastric bypass. Let's accept reality, do an intervention, and get prepped for surgery.

Ye Cannot Serve Both Love and Hate

"The shooter is Mormon," I texted my husband the moment I learned the man who'd killed five and injured eighteen at a Colorado Springs LGBTQ bar was a member of The Church of Jesus Christ of Latter-day Saints.

My husband texted a single word back a moment later. "Arggg!"

After writing the first book on the Upstairs Lounge fire, an arson at a French Quarter gay bar that killed thirty-two people in 1973, I react to news of bar deaths with an added degree of horror. Happy Land. The Station. Pulse.

Regina Adams, a trans woman from my ward, was one of the survivors of the Upstairs fire. Her partner was not so lucky.

My husband and I both served full-time LDS missions in Italy. After we returned to the States, Gary was ordered by his bishop to undergo electroshock torture. I was ordered to meet with an ex-gay therapist.

We chose love instead.

We were both excommunicated.

As the years went by, we listened to continued hateful rhetoric from LDS leaders and LDS politicians. We watched the repulsive Prop 8 campaign. We rolled our eyes over the Proclamation on the Family. Yet we still managed to be shocked by the "November Policy" of 2015 barring church ordinances from children of LGBTQ parents.

Then a couple of weeks ago, we saw LDS Church leaders come out in support of marriage equality.

I was surprised to realize the news left no emotional impact on me. There had *never* been any reason the LDS Church couldn't have maintained its own rules governing 16,000,000+ members and let LGBTQ folks who weren't members live their own lives, the way Mormons already do for folks who drink coffee, wear sleeveless shirts, or watch R-rated movies.

This new policy of "compassion" was such a no-brainer that it was difficult to feel overly excited. Basic human decency, after all, is a pretty low bar for a prophet of God.

And then came the Colorado Springs shooting at Club Q and the glib, smug reactions from right-wing figures.

When news of the Upstairs Lounge fire first reached the residents of New Orleans, many joked about the "weenie roast" in the French Quarter. After churches refused to bury the dead because of their orientation, people joked that they should be buried instead in "fruit jars."

When I told my LDS cousin I was researching the fire, she wrinkled her nose in disgust and said, "You're writing about people who died in a *bar*?"

In recent months, with right-wing religious and political leaders working hard to deny gender-affirming care, trans advocates have pointed out that this oppression will increase suicide rates.

It's an ineffective argument because many of these right-wing leaders are perfectly fine with such an outcome. Those who drive youths to suicide don't even need absolution from Jesus. They're well-practiced at absolving themselves.

As a Mormon, I saw parents, teachers, and leaders teaching young people to hate LGBTQ folks. I saw my fellow congregants laugh at gay men dying of AIDS. And I see many religious conservatives now happy when someone else's kid kills gay or trans folks.

Or when "real men" attack Drag Queen Story Hour. When "patriots" threaten to bomb a Children's Hospital.

Our hands are clean, we tell ourselves. We publicly deny responsibility, but in our hearts, we fully understand we're responsible for "cleansing the world" in preparation for the Second Coming and we're *proud* we did our part.

A basic law of physics is that an object in motion will stay in motion, unless acted upon by an external force. But inertia can also control a mindset and a culture.

A single good decision by LDS leaders can't counteract hundreds of awful ones any more than a single hand pushing against a locomotive can make a train barreling toward a crossing stop the instant someone walks onto the tracks. Prophets and apostles can't eliminate the animosity, disdain, and hatred they've created among their followers simply by saying one or two nice things. Not after decades of preaching animosity, disdain, and hatred.

One of Matthew Shepard's murderers was a Mormon. An Eagle Scout.

I remember one of my zone leaders in Naples attacking a gay couple riding a Vespa.

As a stake missionary in New Orleans, I heard two missionaries discussing a gay member: "Homosexuality must be next to murder."

No. What *is* next to murder is teaching animosity, disdain, and hatred.

If it's true that we cannot serve both God and mammon, it's also true that we cannot serve both love and hate.

LDS leaders have finally come out in support of secular same-sex marriage equality. That's a good thing. But it's going to take far more than that to stop the 16,000,000-car train full of hatred they already set in motion.

When I heard about the shooting in Colorado Springs, I was angry and heartbroken and scared.

But when I learned that the alleged shooter was a member of the LDS Church, all I could feel was absolute and utter disgust.

Guess who taught me that?

You Can't Go Home Again, Even If You've Never Left

Having lived two years in Italy decades ago, I fell in love with European programming when I discovered MHz a few years back. Naturally, I watched lots of French and German and Swedish shows, too, but mostly, I loved watching everything Italian I could find. And while it was as rejuvenating as a cold aranciata during ferragosto, watching the shows was unsettling, too.

Italy had changed a great deal in forty years.

My reaction helps me understand what so many white Americans chanting "Make America Great Again!" are feeling.

The Italy I knew was full of corruption. The streets of Rome were dirty, those in Naples filthy beyond description. Two of my friends lived in a one-room apartment without a bathroom. They had a bucket behind a curtain. Once, I inadvertently walked into a Camorra gang war. Another time, a middle-aged woman pulled me into her apartment to watch the news—the Pope had just been shot.

The Italy I knew was far from perfect. Very, very far.

But while there I discovered the practicality of public transit—buses, metros, light rail, trams, ferries, even a funicolare.

I discovered friendly strangers who welcomed me to their dinner table after only a two-minute chat. I discovered fresh mozzarella, real bread, Nutella.

A middle-aged woman gave me a sweater on a cold winter day. A destitute elderly woman shared her last bit of sour milk. A heterosexual Italian roommate held my hand and kissed me goodnight.

When we hear mostly white Americans say they want to Make America Great Again, we assume they want Jim Crow laws, they want LGBTQ folks back in the closet or even prison, they want women pregnant and trapped in their marriages. Perhaps they even long for a return of slavery.

Some most likely do.

But I think many others just want a return to familiarity, despite a full awareness of its failings.

When I watch Italian TV shows, I see Livia and Salvo mourn the death of a Tunisian boy they almost adopted. I watch Sophia Loren in *The Life Ahead* as a Jewish Holocaust survivor who takes in a Senegalese orphan. Don Matteo in a charming mountain village proves one Filipino immigrant innocent of attempted murder while urging another Filipino immigrant to confess. *Song of Napoli* shows the Napoli I know…but with a female African-Italian police officer. *Lampedusa* reveals the absolute horrors of illegal immigration and its impact on everyone involved.

This isn't the Italy I knew!

I miss gettoni to make phone calls. I miss lire. I miss the life I led forty years ago that wasn't anchored to cell phones and computers.

But you know what? That life doesn't exist anymore. Not for Italians, not for Americans, not for folks in any developed nation or even for many folks in developing nations.

I'm diabetic now and can't even eat Nutella anymore. Or bread. Or pasta.

When I lived in Italy for two years, I was a Mormon missionary. My experience of the country was *never* representative.

But that can really be said of what many conservative white Christian Americans are experiencing now. They were always only a portion of this nation. When I was a missionary, missionary life was the norm, regardless of what my neighbors were doing.

When I watch another episode of *Imma Tataranni* or *The Bastards of Pizzofalcone*, I simultaneously feel a deep longing to exist in that world *and* recognize it as a world I never knew, nothing like the culture and life I experienced at the time.

These new cultural realities in Italy are problematic for everyone. It's easy to see the new problems as worse than the old problems. Both sets of problems, of course, were and are awful. The answer isn't to deport every immigrant, ban cell phones, and pretend the last forty years never happened.

At best, we'd just end up with the horrific problems of forty years ago.

But even that morally questionable goal simply isn't feasible.

Even in what is *my* 1980 nostalgic Italy, there were Italians longing for pre-1966 Italy before Mormons were allowed to proselytize.

Life goes on.

Culture changes.

People immigrate.

Wars and famine and climate change happen.

So…how *do* we deal with all the cultural changes around us? We see some folks acting like cornered animals, raging against anyone who approaches even to help. It's an honest reaction we can't dismiss.

But when we can, let's point out better solutions. Most of the economic fears generated by demographic changes can be addressed by establishing universal healthcare, tuition-free college and vocational training, fare-free public transit, subsidized childcare, and immediate action to begin adapting to what is now inevitable climate disruption.

Pretending that punishing people, depriving others of their rights, and making life miserable for those we don't like will in any way recreate an imperfect past is a losing strategy.

The only workable solution is to use taxpayer money and government power to ensure a well-educated, well-trained population with full access to healthcare, housing, and food. Anything less gives us *Fontamara* and *The Bicycle Thief.*

And that's not a world any of us should want, anywhere.

I Give Gays a Bad Name

I give gays a bad name.

I don't mean to, of course. When I was growing up, my mom kept a notebook about my personality, entering information like "Hates getting his hands dirty," "He likes playing with toy trucks and singing," "Took off his diaper and potty-trained himself," and "He doesn't like being told what to do."

I made A's and B's in school and was moved into Honors classes. I placed third in New Orleans in Typing, second in the state of Louisiana in English.

I was the only boy in my high school Christian club. After graduating, I volunteered two years as a full-time Mormon missionary in Italy.

I was still a virgin at 26.

But one day, a friend introduced me to gay bars.

Mind you, that was thirty-five years ago, and I've still never had a single alcoholic drink. I've never smoked or done recreational drugs.

Naturally, just being gay was enough to get me excommunicated from the LDS Church. After a brief tribunal in a Court of Love, I was ordered to take off my Mormon underwear. And I did strip down…for Show and Tell at a Third Thursday meeting of gay professionals who'd never seen LDS "garments" before. Obviously, my bishop thought I gave Mormons a bad name, but how is it that I give *gays* one, too?

Well, I have a lot of raunchy sex.

I suppose I should amend that. I'm in my sixties now. I *used to* engage in plenty of raunchy sex, and I still have desires and opinions on sex that make even some open-minded gays send disapproving looks my way.

It's difficult to know how much of this grows out of my innate personality and how much is a result of coming out in the French Quarter of New Orleans. There was the Great American Refuge, a piano bar where I listened to Barbra Streisand music one Mardi Gras before heading back to a hotel room with a complete stranger, an ER doc who also turned out to be a former Mormon missionary. Sam and I became fuck buddies, and I recklessly gave him a blow job one day while he drove me to his rural home in Gonzales.

There was the Monster on North Rampart, where some of us from the Gay Men's Chorus would gather after rehearsal on Tuesday night.

There was the Mint on Esplanade where I watched Ricky Graham perform. After Lucille Ball died, he did a skit about Lucy in heaven. "Ethel! Ethel! Help me! I've stolen John Wayne's wings!"

There was the Bourbon Pub, next to the apartment of a deaf man unfazed by the loud music blaring all night long. He was able to fall right asleep after we had sex. I couldn't even doze, but admiring the beautiful nude man beside me the rest of the evening wasn't the worst thing in the world, either.

There was Rawhide, where I met a visiting Jewish ACT UP activist who spit in my face and gave me a hickey every time we had sex in his hotel room. I liked Charles, even went to a protest he organized in front of City Hall before he died.

There was Café Lafitte in Exile, where I stood on the balcony Mardi Gras afternoons dangling beads for the men down on Bourbon Street who showed me their dicks.

There was the dive on North Rampart where I worked up the nerve to ask out Paul, one of the dancers atop the bar, surprising even myself when he agreed.

There was a country and western bar on St. Claude, where I could line dance with Chris, a former Catholic priest.

And there were the Round Up and Good Friends and the Golden Lantern and Corner Pocket and Mississippi River Bottom. That one was next to the leather shop where I bought my first leather vest and chaps.

Those came in handy when I started hanging out at Jewel's on Decatur and the Phoenix on Elysian Fields. Especially after Alan, my boss at the gay bookstore, paid for my nipple piercing.

I lived just a few blocks from the Phoenix, so it became my neighborhood hangout. Even on nights when I wasn't particularly in the mood for cruising, or even up to tolerating thick cigarette smoke, I forced myself to head over. "How many gay men would sell their father's right testicle for a chance to live this close to a gay bar?" I'd tell myself.

I experienced enough life at the Phoenix to fill a book. For one thing, it was where I learned to play pool, which came in handy years later when I was assigned by Jewish Family Services to play pool with an elderly shut-in. It was at the Phoenix where I watched drag shows for the title of Miss Upper Schwegmann Heights, where a tubby man wearing a wig and an apron body-slammed pizza dough on stage for the talent portion of the contest. The same stage would host a leather contest another night.

The Phoenix was where I met Lee, with his XXY chromosomes (Kleinfelter syndrome), where I met George, a university professor from out of state, who enjoyed long kissing sessions when in town but nothing more, where I met Chayim, an ultra-Orthodox leather Jew with whom I briefly studied Talmud.

A dimly lit room upstairs allowed for groping and more. I could smile at a guy, get down on my knees, and let him unzip for me, while listening to the sound of fucking off in the dark corners.

Near the pool table in the main bar, a tourist intrigued by my chaps invited himself home with me. Once there, it turned out he was into pain. Since I wasn't, I suggested we head up to my neighbor's apartment. Ron had a dungeon containing several cots filled with men being fisted. I left the young man with some new friends and returned to my apartment alone.

My headboard was three feet from the buzzer leading up the stairwell to Ron's apartment. Every weekend for years, I'd hear that buzzer ringing again and again throughout the night, followed by the sound of heavy footsteps clomping up the stairs. I never minded being awakened because I felt such contentment knowing other people were having a good time, even if they were doing things I wasn't into myself.

There were other bars, too, the Country Club downriver in the Bywater, with a jukebox playing "Walking to New Orleans." My father, a contractor, had helped build Fats Domino's home not far away in the Lower Ninth ward. After I came out, Dad surprised me by revealing he'd been a Little Richard fan as a teen.

Often embarrassed by me, he loved the patchwork quilt I designed for him of a man plowing a field in his tractor.

The Country Club offered a swimming pool for water polo and a hot tub where I played footsie with a man who'd survived an encounter with the Hammer Killer, a mysterious gay basher never caught who'd attacked several other gay men.

The Country Club was also where Francesca worked, a 40-something British woman who was severely burned in a house fire after going home at the end of her shift. A gay neighbor heard her screams and broke in to rescue her. The regulars at the bar donated clothing and furniture to help get her back on her feet, the bar owners keeping her job open until she could return.

These bars shaped my understanding of gay life, but I realize such a wide and varied experience isn't the norm for most gay men in the U.S. And bars weren't the only influence that turned me into the kind of man who often embarrasses other gays.

There was the bathhouse on Toulouse, with its cubicles and showers and hot tubs, with its St. Andrew's cross and sling, with its glory holes and nude sunbathing on the roof. It was the place where I participated in a Circle Jerk club, where I learned saunas were too miserably hot for sex, where I was first asked to piss inside another man's ass. But it was also where I paid for a gym membership and worked myself into the best physical shape of my life.

Even just living in the Marigny was like living inside a gay bar. Whenever I was in the mood, I could sit on my front steps reading a book, and some guy driving by would pull over, walk up to me, and nod. He'd come in, we'd have sex, and he'd leave, all sometimes without a single word spoken between us.

Is it any wonder I ended up writing books like *Sex among the Saints*, *Sex on the Sabbath*, *Have Your Cum and Eat It, Too*, and *Orgy at the STD Clinic*? It is any wonder I started designing pornographic patchwork quilts?

Things that horrified even some of my closest gay friends.

Is it any wonder I started working as an escort at the age of forty?

Yes, I'm one of those men who give gays a bad name.

As a former Mormon, there's always part of me that feels just a tad inappropriate when I ask a man to shoot onto his partner's asshole so I can lick up his cum. I'm fully aware I do things not all gay men like, things that would give certain right-wing pundits power to further demonize LGBTQ folks.

At the same time, these experiences allowed me to work in an adult gay video store at the age of sixty and offer advice to newbies on how to bottom for the first time. Even nervous men feel comfortable around me because I talk about sex so casually.

As an escort, even as a clerk in a video store, I feel I performed more genuine service than I ever did as a missionary.

Enjoying sex, of course, doesn't mean that's all I think about. I'm also a union steward who advocates for the rights of my coworkers. I write about climate breakdown and universal healthcare. I advocate for tuition-free college and vocational training. I enjoy reading a good gay murder mystery. And I sing along with music videos.

Francesco Gabbani has some damn good songs.

My husband of fifteen years and I watch European TV shows most evenings. *The Vicar of Dibley* out of the UK, *Annika Bengtzon: Crime Reporter* out of Sweden, *Fractures* out of Iceland, *Tatort: Weimar* out of Germany, *Midnight at the Pera Palace* out of Turkey. *Masantonio*, *La Porta Rossa*, and *Petra* out of Italy. Gary, after all, did his Mormon mission in Italy, too.

I bought him a leather sling for our first anniversary.

In addition to my DNA and upbringing, many other things have shaped my attitude about sexuality, toward life in general. Some of the biggest influences, though, were those liberating French Quarter gay bars.

I feel so, so lucky to have had them.

Do Good People Smile Behind Closed Doors When LGBTQ Folks Are Murdered?

When you heard about a shooter killing five people in a Colorado Springs LGBTQ bar, were you happy or upset?

When you learned the alleged shooter was a member of The Church of Jesus Christ of Latter-day Saints, were you proud or embarrassed? If you were embarrassed, was it because of what "the world" might think? Was your embarrassment a matter of PR or do you believe the man committed a horrific sin?

Are you a good witch or a bad witch?

I can't help but make a *Wizard of Oz* reference. LGBTQ folks see the world through oppression-colored glasses. Many of my former friends and family consider themselves righteous, faithful followers of Jesus Christ. They're so good, in fact, they can't bear to associate with me any longer.

I'm gay, after all. If cleanliness is next to godliness, homosexuality is next to devil worship.

Every February 5, I remember the day of my baptism. Every September 4, I remember the day I entered the Missionary Training Center. Every November 4, I remember the day I first arrived in Rome to work as a full-time Mormon missionary.

The truth is that most of the right-wing pundits, politicians, and religious leaders who say the terrible things that inevitably lead to murder *wanted* the outcome in Colorado Springs. The attack wasn't an unfortunate accident because some "crazy" person "misunderstood" or "took things too far."

Most of these folks are barely hiding their excitement or are even openly gleeful at the result. Whether or not they say so in public, they're exhilarated their hateful words succeeded in bringing about the death of LGBTQ people and their allies. This latest killing won't shock them into realizing the error of their ways. They see that their ways—hatred and lies—work to achieve their goal. They aren't backing away from that rhetoric *because they want the slaughter to keep happening.*

Unless *you* also want that same outcome, you can't wait for the people you've admired for years to change their messaging and allow you to stop wishing for and encouraging murder. Lying for the Lord is still lying. Hating for the Lord is still hating.

Murdering for the Lord is still murdering. That's problematic, of course, because LDS scriptures do condone murder. We might take this opportunity then to also reconsider whether or not such doctrine constitutes a problem with our canon. It was LDS leaders, after all, who gave us LDS scripture. Will we keep following blindly even when asked to lie, hate, and kill?

I remember going through the temple for the first time and consenting to have my throat slit, consenting to disembowelment, if I ever revealed the secret handshakes allowing faithful Mormons access to heaven. Everyone present blithely agreed to the same atrocities.

Recently, leaders of the LDS Church came out in support of marriage equality, finally acknowledging that they are perfectly free to tell their own members how to live while still granting the right of non-Mormons to make major life choices for themselves.

This is good, even if LGBTQ folks and our allies are naturally suspicious, given the vitriol from Spencer W. Kimball, Boyd K. Packer, and many others, given the Prop 8 campaign, the Proclamation on the Family, and the 2015 Exclusion Policy barring children of LGBTQ parents from baptism and other church ordinances.

LDS leaders have treated their church like a High Sierra forest during increasingly arid conditions, planting shrubs and wildflowers and young trees that soon wither, until the forest is filled with dry kindling in the midst of a record drought. It doesn't even matter who tosses the match. Right-wing leaders of all types have created the conditions ripe for an explosive fire.

Were *you* one of those people cracking gay jokes at church? Did you teach the youth that gay men and trans women are abominations?

Were you secretly hoping that someone else's kid would do the world a favor by killing some of these undesirables? Or did you merely hope to teach LGBTQ kids self-loathing, believing that alone was enough of a good deed?

Words lead to thoughts which lead to actions. We preach this principle when encouraging our youth to remain stalwart. But that same pipeline exists when preaching hatred, disdain, and condemnation.

If "I was just following orders" didn't work at Nuremburg, do we think it will work on Judgment Day?

Do we *ever* need to take responsibility for our own words, actions, and attitudes when they push someone else to murder the objects of our repulsion?

Are we aiding and abetting? Are we accomplices? Co-conspirators?

If *you* think murdering LGBTQ folks is doing God's will, there's no conversation to be had. But if you think it's wrong, it's time to take stock.

Latter-day Saints, Christians of all denominations, and the faithful of every religion who believe in "family values" must take a stand. There's no fence-sitting here. No lukewarm shrug. You've found yourselves, wittingly or not, on the side of hate. Is that what you intended? Or do you now realize you were led astray despite your sincere faith?

In the wake of these latest killings, almost all right-wing pundits and preachers are doubling down on their hate. Is that what *you're* going to do as well?

They won’t change their minds.

Will you?

I'm Spending My Children's Inheritance

Imagine you're fifty-five years old. Not elderly. Not young. But you could have had another twenty or thirty good years ahead. Only you don't. You've just been diagnosed with stage 4, terminal cancer.

As a reasonably moral person, how would you react? How would any of us?

Our decision will determine what we do in the face of devastating climate change.

When I was a child, I was shocked to discover that people facing death didn't suddenly become nicer, more righteous. They were about to meet God, after all. Didn't they at least want to squeeze in a few extra bonus points?

Barring a brain injury from an accident or disease, however, our personalities remain consistent as we near the end.

Some people distribute their favorite possessions before they go to make sure the items end up in the hands of folks who will appreciate them.

Others refuse to leave a will. "I don't care what happens to people after I die," one of my partners told me when he was diagnosed with liver cancer.

As hurtful as those words were, they were still better than what many people are doing now—selling off their family's possessions, stealing from their neighbors, and embezzling the retirement funds of others, just so they can have one last, great, fun party.

They're owners of the Triangle Shirtwaist Factory exiting a burning building while leaving their employees locked inside.

People in my family, religious conservatives of many types, and corporate Democrats, desperate to enjoy life to the fullest, are taking out massive loans after forging their children's and grandchildren's signatures, almost as if they believe they're casting a magic spell that can stop normal biological processes, as if they think they can cast a spell on God himself.

That's not how any of this works.

When climate activists demand we use nuclear energy instead of fossil fuels, I realize they don't really get it, either. Sure, nuclear energy, despite its natural problems, *might* be a reasonable alternative as we transition, but that technology has one major, inescapable flaw.

It must coexist with humans.

Humans attack and fight. They sabotage and bomb.

Humans scrimp and save on costs. They cut corners.

And humans make unintentional, human mistakes.

We aren't compatible with nuclear facilities, no matter how well meaning 95% of us are.

I'm an old, fat man with multiple medical issues. I don't have an impending death sentence yet. Other than the knowledge that I'm mortal and nearing the end of my time here, even under the best of circumstances.

I've already given away most of my prized possessions, living simply and trying to enjoy whatever time I have left.

I have no children, no grandchildren. I *could* choose not to care about the people still here after I'm gone.

But that would mean changing my personality at this advanced stage of my life. Even if I could, I wouldn't be trying to become *worse*.

It's clear we must drastically and quickly reduce our use of fossil fuels to avoid the worst effects of climate change. Horrendous consequences are already inevitable because of folks who insist on extending their wild, expensive party as long as they can.

That includes everyone who claims profits are more important than a survivable climate. Everyone who willfully chooses to ignore the thousands of reports proving the problem is a real, existential threat.

We can debate the best ways to move forward but building new projects to extract and burn fossil fuels cannot be on the table.

Imagine we're in the audience of a talk show, and the host excitedly announces a surprise gift for each of us. "*You* get a stage 4 cancer diagnosis, and *you* get a stage 4 cancer diagnosis! *Everyone* gets a stage 4 cancer diagnosis!"

That's the situation we're in. Humans may not go completely extinct, but civilization, even in a best-case scenario, will be lost. And there are a good many projections that suggest it's already too late to do *anything* to save ourselves.

So we're at the end of our life. What do we do?

We can take an experimental treatment and try to survive—drastic climate action—or we can spend the remainder of our days…how?

Being kind to our friends and family?

Spending our last seconds gouging neighbors for one more dollar of profit?

Perhaps we can slap a bumper sticker on our shiny, brand-new gas guzzler: "I'm spending my children's inheritance!"

The answer to the question of our existential morality depends on what kind of person we are.

So, whatever stage of denial you may be in right now, you'll ultimately have to ask the question. What kind of person are *you*?

Acknowledgement of Previous Publication

"Are We 'Catastrophizing' if We're Really in a Catastrophe?" published in *LA Progressive* on January 31, 2022

"Be a Jerk for Jesus," published in *LA Progressive* on August 9, 2022

"Can We At Least Get a Proxy Apology?" published in *LA Progressive* on May 21, 2022

"Climate Inaction in Action," published in *LA Progressive* on May 3, 2022

"Coats When It's Cold, Masks When There's Virus," published in the *Salt Lake Tribune* on July 21, 2022

"Compassion Seattle's Lack of Compassion," published in *LA Progressive* on July 29, 2021

"COVID Analogies Are the New Holocaust Analogies," published in *LA Progressive* on August 15, 2021

"Disdain for the Deluded," published in *LA Progressive* on July 12, 2021

"Do Good People Smile Behind Closed Doors When LGBTQ Folks Are Murdered?" published in *Main Street Plaza* on November 25, 2022

"Do You Smell Smoke?" published in *LA Progressive* on May 31, 2022

"Every Newscast Must Discuss Climate," published in *LA Progressive* on January 26, 2022

"Football Has Fans, Religion Exists, and Climate Change Is Real, Too," published in *LA Progressive* on December 16, 2022

"From Book Burner to Librarian," published in *LA Progressive* on February 15, 2022

"A Gastric Bypass for Global Warming," published in *LA Progressive* on July 28, 2022

"Go Fund Yourself!" published in *LA Progressive* on Dec 14, 2021

"I Don't Use Pronouns," published in *LA Progressive* on April 20, 2022

"I'm a Diabetic Afraid of Needles, and I'm Triple-Vaxxed," published in the *Salt Lake Tribune* on Jan 7, 2022

"I'm My Own Grandchild," published in *LA Progressive* on July 15, 2021

"I'm Spending My Children's Inheritance," published in *LA Progressive* on May 23, 2022

"Is There Anything I Can Say to Get You to Donate?" published in *LA Progressive* on August 1, 2022

"Let's Celebrate Higher Gas Prices," published in *LA Progressive* on March 11, 2022

"Let's Change Our Attitude Toward Race," published in *LA Progressive* on June 24, 2021

"Make Christians Christlike Again," published in *LA Progressive* on March 10, 2022

"Moral Snobbery, Snarky Comments, and Mockery Rarely Win Converts," published in *LA Progressive* on January 13, 2022

"Parents Who Believe in Sexual Purity Should Still Vaccinate Their Kids Against HPV," published in *Main Street Plaza* on February 14, 2022

"The Party That Cried Wolf," published in *LA Progressive* on January 17, 2022

"Pro-Corporate Programming as 'Feel Good' Drama," published in *Hollywood Progressive* on Dec 23, 2021

"*Second Thought*: An Introductory Socialist YouTube Channel," published in *LA Progressive* on December 5, 2022

"Stop Moderate-Splaining!" published in *LA Progressive* on February 26, 2022

"Student Loans Create Chronic Stress," published in *LA Progressive* on Sept 5, 2021

"A Tale of Two Parties," published in *LA Progressive* on Dec 15, 2021

"This Isn't the New Normal. These Are the Good Old Days," published in *LA Progessive* on September 13, 2022

"Weekend and Holiday Transit Schedules Hurt the Most Vulnerable Riders," published in *LA Progressive* on Nov 29, 2021

"We Must Adjust to a Changing World," published in the *Salt Lake Tribune* on July 1, 2021

"Will Capitalism Reign During the Millennium?" published in *Main Street Plaza* on September 25, 2022

"The World's Most Extraordinary Income Inequality," published in *LA Progressive* on January 14, 2022

"Workers Quitting Crappy Jobs Should Also Quit Crappy Political Parties," published in *LA Progressive* on Nov 6, 2021

"Ye Cannot Serve Both Love and Hate," published in the *Salt Lake Tribune* on November 26, 2022

"Yes, I'm Offended and I Want to Sin," published in the *Salt Lake Tribune* on August 21, 2022

"You Can't Go Home Again, Even If You've Never Left," published in *LA Progressive* on May 4, 2022

Books by Johnny Townsend

Thanks for reading! If you enjoyed this book, could you please take a few minutes to write a review online? Reviews are helpful both to me as an author and to other readers, so we'd all sincerely appreciate your writing one! And if you did enjoy the book, here are some others I've written you might want to look up:

Mormon Underwear

God's Gargoyles

The Circumcision of God

Sex among the Saints

Dinosaur Perversions

Zombies for Jesus

The Abominable Gayman

The Gay Mormon Quilter's Club

The Golem of Rabbi Loew

Mormon Fairy Tales

Flying over Babel

Marginal Mormons

Mormon Bullies

The Mormon Victorian Society

Dragons of the Book of Mormon

Selling the City of Enoch

A Day at the Temple

Behind the Zion Curtain

Gayrabian Nights

Lying for the Lord

Despots of Deseret

Missionaries Make the Best Companions

Invasion of the Spirit Snatchers

The Tyranny of Silence

Sex on the Sabbath

The Washing of Brains

The Mormon Inquisition

Interview with a Mission President

Weeping, Wailing, and Gnashing of Teeth

Behind the Bishop's Door

The Moat around Zion

The Last Days Linger

Mormon Madness

Human Compassion for Beginners

Dead Mankind Walking

Who Invited You to the Orgy?

Breaking the Promise of the Promised Land

I Will, Through the Veil

Am I My Planet's Keeper?

Have Your Cum and Eat It, Too

Strangers with Benefits

What Would Anne Frank Do?

This Is All Just Too Hard

Glory to the Glory Hole!

My Pre-Bucket List

Blessed Are the Firefighters

Wake Up and Smell the Missionaries

Quilting Beyond the Rainbow

Gay Sleeping Arrangements

Queer Quilting

Racism by Proxy

Orgy at the STD Clinic

Life Is Better with Love

Please Evacuate

Recommended Daily Humanity

Let the Faggots Burn: The UpStairs Lounge Fire

Latter-Gay Saints: An Anthology of Gay Mormon Fiction (co-editor)

Available from your favorite online or neighborhood bookstore.

Wondering what some of those other books are about? Read on!

Invasion of the Spirit Snatchers

During the Apocalypse, a group of Mormon survivors in Hurricane, Utah gather in the home of the Relief Society president, telling stories to pass the time as they ration their food storage and await the Second Coming. But this is no ordinary group of Mormons—or perhaps it is. They are the faithful, feminist, gay, apostate, and repentant, all working together to help each other through the darkest days any of them have yet seen.

Gayrabian Nights

Gayrabian Nights is a twist on the well-known classic, *1001 Arabian Nights*, in which Scheherazade, under the threat of death if she ceases to captivate King Shahryar's attention, enchants him through a series of mysterious, adventurous, and romantic tales.

In this variation, a male escort, invited to the hotel room of a closeted, homophobic Mormon senator, learns that the man is poised to vote on a piece of anti-gay legislation the following morning. To prevent him from sleeping, so that the exhausted senator will miss casting his vote on the Senate floor, the escort entertains him with stories of homophobia, celibacy, mixed orientation marriages, reparative therapy, coming out, first love, gay marriage, and long-term successful gay relationships. The escort crafts the stories to give the senator a crash course in gay culture and sensibilities, hoping to bring the man closer to accepting his own sexual orientation.

Let the Faggots Burn: The UpStairs Lounge Fire

On Gay Pride Day in 1973, someone set the entrance to a French Quarter gay bar on fire. In the terrible inferno that followed, thirty-two people lost their lives, including a third of the local congregation of the Metropolitan Community Church, their pastor burning to death halfway out a second-story window as he tried to claw his way to freedom. A mother who'd gone to the bar with her two gay sons died alongside them. A man who'd helped his friend escape first was found dead near the fire escape. Two children waited outside a movie theater across town for a father and step-father who would never pick them up. During this era of rampant homophobia, several families refused to claim the bodies, and many churches refused to bury the dead. Author Johnny Townsend pored through old records and tracked down survivors of the fire as well as relatives and friends of those killed to compile this fascinating account of a forgotten moment in gay history.

The Abominable Gayman

What is a gay Mormon missionary doing in Italy? He is trying to save his own soul as well as the souls of others.

In these tales chronicling the two-year mission of Robert Anderson, we see a young man tormented by his inability to be the man the Church says he should be. In addition to his personal hell, Anderson faces a major earthquake, organized crime, a serious bus accident, and much more. He copes with horrendous mission leaders and his own suicidal tendencies. But one day, he meets another missionary who loves him, and his world changes forever.

Missionaries Make the Best Companions

What lies behind the freshly scrubbed façades of the Mormon missionaries we see about town? In these stories, an ex-Mormon tries to seduce a faithful elder by showing him increasingly suggestive movies. A sister missionary fulfills her community service requirement by babysitting for a prostitute. Two elders break their mission rules by venturing into the forbidden French Quarter. A senior missionary couple try to reactivate lapsed members while their own family falls apart back home. A young man hopes that serving a second full-time mission will lead him up the Church hierarchy. Two bored missionaries decide to make a little extra money moonlighting in a male stripper club. Two frustrated elders find an acceptable way to masturbate—by donating to a Fertility Clinic. A lonely man searches for the favorite companion he hasn't seen in thirty years.

The Golem of Rabbi Loew

Jacob and Esau Cohen are the closest of brothers. In fact, they're lovers. A doctor tries to combine canine genes with those of Jews, to improve their chances of surviving a hostile world. A Talmudic scholar dates an escort. A scientist tries to develop the "God spot" in the brains of his patients in order to create a messiah. The Golem of Prague is really Rabbi Loew's secret lover. While some of the Jews in Townsend's book are Orthodox, this collection of Jewish stories most certainly is not.

The Last Days Linger

The scriptures tell us that in the Last Days, wickedness will increase upon the Earth. When leaders of the Mormon Church see a rise in the number of gay members, they believe the end is upon them. But while "wickedness never was happiness," it begins to appear that wickedness can sometimes be divine. At least, the stories here suggest that religious proscriptions condemning homosexuality have it all wrong. While gay Mormons may be no closer to perfection than anyone else, they're no further from it, either. And sometimes, being gay provides just the right ingredient to create saints—as flawed as God himself.

Mormon Madness

Mental illness can strike the faithful as easily as anyone else. But often religious doctrine and practice exacerbate rather than alleviate these problems. From schizophrenia to obsessive-compulsive disorder, from persecution complex to sexual dysfunction, autism to dissociative identity disorder, Mormons must cope with their mental as well as their spiritual health on a daily basis.

Am I My Planet's Keeper?

Global Warming. Climate Change. Climate Crisis. Climate Emergency. Whatever label we use, we are facing one of the greatest challenges to the survival of life as we know it.

But while addressing greenhouse gases is perhaps our most urgent need, it's not our only task. We must also address toxic waste, pollution, habitat destruction, and our other contributions to the world's sixth mass extinction event.

In order to do that, we must simultaneously address the unmet human needs that keep us distracted from deeper engagement in stabilizing our climate: moderating economic inequality, guaranteeing healthcare to all, and ensuring education for everyone.

And to accomplish *that*, we must unite to combat the monied forces that use fear, prejudice, and misinformation to manipulate us.

It's a daunting task. But success is our only option.

Wake Up and Smell the Missionaries

Two Mormon missionaries in Italy discover they share the same rare ability—both can emit pheromones on demand. At first, they playfully compete in the hills of Frascati to see who can tempt "investigators" most. But soon they're targeting each other non-stop.

Can two immature young men learn to control their "superpower" to live a normal life…and develop genuine love? Even as their relationship is threatened by the attentions of another man?

They seem just on the verge of success when a massive earthquake leaves them trapped under the rubble of their apartment in Castellammare.

With night falling and temperatures dropping, can they dig themselves out in time to save themselves? And will their injuries destroy the ability that brought them together in the first place?

Orgy at the STD Clinic

Todd Tillotson is struggling to move on after his husband is killed in a hit and run attack a year earlier during a Black Lives Matter protest in Seattle.

In this novel set entirely on public transportation, we watch as Todd, isolated throughout the pandemic, battles desperation in his attempt to safely reconnect with the world.

Will he find love again, even casual friendship, or will he simply end up another crazy old man on the bus?

Things don't look good until a man whose face he can't even see sits down beside him despite the raging variants.

And asks him a question that will change his life.

Please Evacuate

A gay, partygoing New Yorker unconcerned about the future or the unsustainability of capitalism is hit by a truck and thrust into a straight man's body half a continent away. As Hunter tries to figure out what's happening, he's caught up in another disaster, a wildfire sweeping through a Colorado community, the flames overtaking him and several schoolchildren as they flee.

When he awakens, Hunter finds himself in the body of yet another man, this time in northern Italy, a former missionary about to marry a young Mormon woman. Still piecing together this new reality, and beginning to embrace his latest identity, Hunter fights for his life in a devastating flash flood along with his wife *and* his new husband.

He's an aging worker in drought-stricken Texas, a nurse at an assisted living facility in the direct path of a hurricane, an advocate for the unhoused during a freak Seattle blizzard.

We watch as Hunter is plunged into life after life, finally recognizing the futility of only looking out for #1 and understanding the part he must play in addressing the global climate crisis…if he ever gets another chance.

What Readers Have Said

Townsend's stories are "a gay *Portnoy's Complaint* of Mormonism. Salacious, sweet, sad, insightful, insulting, religiously ethnic, quirky-faithful, and funny."

D. Michael Quinn, author of *The Mormon Hierarchy: Origins of Power*

"Told from a believably conversational first-person perspective, [*The Abominable Gayman*'s] novelistic focus on Anderson's journey to thoughtful self-acceptance allows for greater character development than often seen in short stories, which makes this well-paced work rich and satisfying, and one of Townsend's strongest. An extremely important contribution to the field of Mormon fiction." Named to Kirkus Reviews' Best of 2011.

Kirkus Reviews

"The thirteen stories in *Mormon Underwear* capture this struggle [between Mormonism and homosexuality] with humor, sadness, insight, and sometimes shocking details....*Mormon Underwear* provides compelling stories, literally from the inside-out."

Niki D'Andrea, *Phoenix New Times*

"Townsend's lively writing style and engaging characters [in *Zombies for Jesus*] make for stories which force us to wake up, smell the (prohibited) coffee, and review our attitudes with regard to reading dogma so doggedly. These are tales which revel in the individual tics and quirks which make us human, Mormon or not, gay or not…"

A.J. Kirby, *The Short Review*

"The Rift," from *The Abominable Gayman*, is a "fascinating tale of an untenable situation…a *tour de force*."

David Lenson, editor, *The Massachusetts Review*

"Pronouncing the Apostrophe," from *The Golem of Rabbi Loew*, is "quiet and revealing, an intriguing tale…"

Sima Rabinowitz, Literary Magazine Review, *NewPages.com*

The Circumcision of God is "a collection of short stories that consider the imperfect, silenced majority of Mormons, who may in fact be [the Church's] best hope….[The book leaves] readers regretting the church's willingness to marginalize those who best exemplify its ideals: those who love fiercely despite all obstacles, who brave challenges at great personal risk and who always choose the hard, higher road."

Kirkus Reviews

In *Mormon Fairy Tales*, Johnny Townsend displays "both a wicked sense of irony and a deep well of compassion."

Kel Munger, *Sacramento News and Review*

Zombies for Jesus is "eerie, erotic, and magical."

Publishers Weekly

"While [Townsend's] many touching vignettes draw deeply from Mormon mythology, history, spirituality and culture, [*Mormon Fairy Tales*] is neither a gaudy act of proselytism nor angry protest literature from an ex-believer. Like all good fiction, his stories are simply about the joys, the hopes and the sorrows of people."

Kirkus Reviews

"In *Let the Faggots Burn* author Johnny Townsend restores this tragic event [the UpStairs Lounge fire] to its proper place in LGBT history and reminds us that the victims of the blaze were not just 'statistics,' but real people with real lives, families, and friends."

Jesse Monteagudo, *The Bilerico Project*

In *Let the Faggots Burn,* "Townsend's heart-rending descriptions of the victims…seem to [make them] come alive once more."

Kit Van Cleave, *OutSmart Magazine*

Marginal Mormons is "an irreverent, honest look at life outside the mainstream Mormon Church….Throughout his musings on sin and forgiveness, Townsend beautifully demonstrates his characters' internal, perhaps irreconcilable struggles….Rather than anger and disdain, he offers an honest portrayal of people searching for meaning and community in their lives, regardless of their life choices or secrets." Named to Kirkus Reviews' Best of 2012.

Kirkus Reviews

The stories in *The Mormon Victorian Society* "register the new openness and confidence of gay life in the age of same-sex marriage….What hasn't changed is Townsend's wry, conversational prose, his subtle evocations of character and social dynamics, and his deadpan humor. His warm empathy still glows in this intimate yet clear-eyed engagement with Mormon theology and folkways. Funny, shrewd and finely wrought dissections of the awkward contradictions—and surprising harmonies—between conscience and desire." Named to Kirkus Reviews' Best of 2013.

Kirkus Reviews

"This collection of short stories [*The Mormon Victorian Society*] featuring gay Mormon characters slammed [me] in the face from the first page, wrestled my heart and mind to the floor, and left me panting and wanting more by the end. Johnny Townsend has created so many memorable characters in such few pages. I went weeks thinking about this book. It truly touched me."

Tom Webb, *A Bear on Books*

Dragons of the Book of Mormon is an "entertaining collection....Townsend's prose is sharp, clear, and easy to read, and his characters are well rendered..."

Publishers Weekly

"The pre-eminent documenter of alternative Mormon lifestyles...Townsend has a deep understanding of his characters, and his limpid prose, dry humor and well-grounded (occasionally magical) realism make their spiritual conundrums both compelling and entertaining. [*Dragons of the Book of Mormon* is] [a]nother of Townsend's critical but affectionate and absorbing tours of Mormon discontent." Named to Kirkus Reviews' Best of 2014.

Kirkus Reviews

In *Gayrabian Nights*, "Townsend's prose is always limpid and evocative, and…he finds real drama and emotional depth in the most ordinary of lives."

Kirkus Reviews

Gayrabian Nights is a "complex revelation of how seriously soul damaging the denial of the true self can be."

Ryan Rhodes, author of *Free Electricity*

Gayrabian Nights "was easily the most original book I've read all year. Funny, touching, topical, and thoroughly enjoyable."

Rainbow Awards

Lying for the Lord is "one of the most gripping books that I've picked up for quite a while. I love the author's writing style, alternately cynical, humorous, biting, scathing, poignant, and touching…. This is the third book of his that I've read, and all are equally engaging. These are stories that need to be told, and the author does it in just the right way."

Heidi Alsop, *Ex-Mormon Foundation Board Member*

In *Lying for the Lord*, Townsend "gets under the skin of his characters to reveal their complexity and conflicts….shrewd, evocative [and] wryly humorous."

Kirkus Reviews

In *Missionaries Make the Best Companions*, "the author treats the clash between religious dogma and liberal humanism with vivid realism, sly humor, and subtle feeling as his characters try to figure out their true missions in life. Another of Townsend's rich dissections of Mormon failures and uncertainties…" Named to Kirkus Reviews' Best of 2015.

Kirkus Reviews

In *Invasion of the Spirit Snatchers*, "Townsend, a confident and practiced storyteller, skewers the hypocrisies and eccentricities of his characters with precision and affection. The outlandish framing narrative is the most consistent source of shock and humor, but the stories do much to ground the reader in the world—or former world—of the characters….A funny, charming tale about a group of Mormons facing the end of the world."

Kirkus Reviews

"Townsend's collection [*The Washing of Brains*] once again displays his limpid, naturalistic prose, skillful narrative chops, and his subtle insights into psychology…Well-crafted dispatches on the clash between religion and self-fulfillment…"

Kirkus Reviews

"While the author is generally at his best when working as a satirist, there are some fine, understated touches in these tales [*The Last Days Linger*] that will likely affect readers in subtle ways….readers should come away impressed by the deep empathy he shows for all his characters—even the homophobic ones."

Kirkus Reviews

"Written in a conversational style that often uses stories and personal anecdotes to reveal larger truths, this immensely approachable book [*Racism by Proxy*] skillfully serves its intended audience of White readers grappling with complex questions regarding race, history, and identity. The author's frequent references to the Church of Jesus Christ of Latter-day Saints may be too niche for readers unfamiliar with its idiosyncrasies, but Townsend generally strikes a perfect balance of humor, introspection, and reasoned arguments that will engage even skeptical readers."

Kirkus Reviews

Orgy at the STD Clinic portrays "an all-too real scenario that Townsend skewers to wincingly accurate proportions…[with] instant classic moments courtesy of his punchy, sassy, sexy lead character…"

Jim Piechota, *Bay Area Reporter*

Orgy at the STD Clinic is "…a triumph of humane sensibility. A richly textured saga that brilliantly captures the fraying social fabric of contemporary life." Named to Kirkus Reviews' Best Indie Books of 2022.

Kirkus Reviews